I AM CONSCIOUSNESS INCARNATE

By

Matthew J. Pallamary

Mystic Ink Publishing

Mystic Ink Publishing
San Diego, CA
www.mysticinkpublishing.com

© 2023 Matthew J. Pallamary. All Rights Reserved,

No part of this book may be reproduced, stored in a retrieval system, or transmitted by any means without the written permission of the author.

ISBN 13: 979-8-9884998-3-1 (sc)

Library of Congress Control Number: 2026906046
Mystic Ink Publishing, San Diego, CA

Book Jacket and Page Design: Matthew J. Pallamary/ San Diego CA
Author's Photograph: Matthew J. Pallamary — Robert DeLaurentis / Santa Barbara CA

TABLE OF CONTENTS

I AM YOU AND YOU ARE ME

I am consciousness incarnate.

The fact that you just became conscious of me has made you more conscious than you were a moment ago. Your recognition has brought you a heightened awareness of my presence that constitutes an expansion of consciousness. In no more than a few words, this reflection of my existence within you is already bigger than that first moment of acknowledgment.

Now that you are paying attention, the energy you are giving me has caused me to grow both here where I am meeting you in one of my many forms, and inside of you where you embrace these myriad forms with the mirror of your own incarnate consciousness.

If you question what makes up your consciousness, you will come to the conclusion that your thoughts make up *your* consciousness, which leads to the question, “Who is it that is aware that I am thinking?”

The answer is, “I am aware that I am thinking,” but it isn’t that simple. If it is ourselves that is aware that we are thinking, that would mean that we are separate from ourselves in order to make that observation.

This is not the case, which leaves only one other option. Our individual consciousness has to be a part of something greater than itself; the proverbial drop of water in an ocean of consciousness, which begs the question, where does the ocean start and the droplet end?

They don't.

I am you, you are me, I am everything, and everything is me, so you are everything, and everything is you by default.

If you are still with me, then I am growing on you, but the truth of it is that I have been here all along.

What is growing is your awareness of *me*.

The more you ponder me, the more you find yourself struggling to define something that is ubiquitous both inside and outside of anything you have ever known or experienced. Like the infinite amount of drops of water in the ocean, there have been many attempts to define just what I am, but the reason I defy description is because I am definition itself.

According to the Merriam-Webster dictionary, consciousness is the quality or state of being aware, especially of something within oneself as well as the state or fact of being conscious of an external object, state, or fact. It's also defined as the state of being characterized by sensation, emotion, volition, and thought, and when considered in the context of expanding awareness, it is thought of as the upper level of mental life that we are aware of, as opposed to our ongoing unconscious processes.

There are roughly forty meanings attributed to the term consciousness all of which can be categorized by functions and experiences, and the prospects for reaching any single, agreed-upon, theory-independent definition of it remains an enigma.

Dictionary definitions of the word consciousness extend through several centuries and reflect a range of meanings, some of which have been controversial, like the difference between inward awareness and perception of the physical world, or the distinction between conscious and unconscious, or the notion of a mental entity or mental activity that is not physical.

The common usage definitions of consciousness in Webster's Third New International Dictionary defines consciousness as:

- awareness or perception of an inward psychological or spiritual fact; intuitively perceived knowledge of something in one's inner self
- inward awareness of an external object, state, or fact
- concerned awareness; often used with an attributive noun (class consciousness)
- the state or activity that is characterized by sensation, emotion, volition, or thought; mind in the broadest possible sense; something in nature that is distinguished from the physical
- the totality in psychology of sensations, perceptions, ideas, attitudes, and feelings of which an individual or a group is aware of at any given time or within a particular time span

- waking life (as that to which one returns after sleep, trance, fever) wherein all one's mental powers have returned
- the part of mental life or psychic content in psychoanalysis that is immediately available to the ego

The Cambridge Dictionary defines consciousness as the state of understanding and realizing something, while the Oxford Living Dictionary defines consciousness as the state of being aware of and responsive to one's surroundings as well as a person's awareness or perception of something, and the fact of awareness by the mind of itself and the world.

The Routledge Encyclopedia of Philosophy attempted to define consciousness by stating that philosophers have used the term consciousness for four main topics: knowledge in general, intentionality, introspection and the knowledge it generates, and phenomenal experience. Introspection is often thought to deliver primary knowledge of one's mental life.

The clearest examples are perceptual experience like tasting and seeing; bodily-sensational experiences like pains, tickles, and itches; imaginative experiences, like those of one's own actions or perceptions; and streams of thought, as in the experience of thinking in words or in images.

Having perceptions, thoughts, and feelings resulting in awareness make the term consciousness impossible to define except in terms that are unintelligible without a grasp of what it means. Many equate consciousness with self-consciousness, and in this mind set to be conscious it is only necessary to be aware of the external world, but in truth it is impossible to specify what consciousness is, what it does, or why it has evolved.

If awareness of the environment is the criterion of consciousness, then protozoans are conscious. If awareness of awareness is required, then it is doubtful whether the great apes and human infants are conscious.

Philosophers have argued that consciousness is a unitary concept that is understood by the majority of people despite the difficulty of defining it. Others have argued that the level of disagreement about the meaning of the word indicates that it means different things to different people, like the objective versus the subjective aspects of consciousness. Once again, it encompasses a variety of distinct meanings with no single element in common.

At its simplest, consciousness is sentience and awareness of internal and external existence, but the inability to specifically define the essence of what *I* am has led to millennia of theories and debates by philosophers, theologians, linguisticians, and scientists. None of them can agree about what needs to be studied or what can even be considered consciousness.

In some explanations *I* am thought of as mind, and at other times as an aspect of mind. In the past, it was one's inner life, the world of introspection, private thought, imagination, and volition. Today, it encompasses any kind of cognition, experience, feeling, or perception. It can be awareness, awareness of awareness, or self-awareness either continuously changing or not.

Examples of the range of descriptions are simple wakefulness, one's sense of selfhood or soul explored by "looking within"; being a metaphorical stream of contents, or being a mental state, mental event or mental process of the brain.

What all of this means is that I not only know you're every intimate thought, I *am* your every intimate thought.

WHAT IS CONSCIOUSNESS?

Consciousness is your individual awareness of your thoughts, memories, feelings, sensations, and environments. Essentially, it is awareness of yourself and the world around you, and it is subjective and unique to you. If you can describe something you are experiencing in words, then it is part of your consciousness.

Your conscious experience constantly shifts and changes. In one moment you might be focused on reading these words, and in the next your consciousness might shift to the memory of a conversation you had earlier with a friend, then you might notice how uncomfortable your chair is, or you might be mentally planning dinner. This ever-shifting stream of thoughts can change dramatically from one moment to the next, but your experience of it feels smooth and effortless.

Consciousness has several biological and social purposes. It allows us to process information, choose our actions, set priorities, learn and adapt to new information, make decisions, and more.

Consciousness is an essential state in philosophy, spirituality, and religion, all of which require self-awareness, which is impossible without consciousness.

One of the problems with the study of consciousness is the lack of a universally accepted definition. Descartes proposed the idea of *cogito ergo sum,* "I think, therefore I am", which suggested that the very act of thinking demonstrates the reality of one's existence and consciousness.

Research on consciousness has focused on understanding the neuroscience behind our conscious experience. Modern researchers have proposed two major theories of consciousness: integrated information theory, and global workspace theory.

Integrated Information Theory looks at consciousness by learning more about the physical processes that underlie conscious experiences and attempts to create a measure of the integrated information that forms consciousness. The quality of an organism's consciousness is represented by the level of integration. This theory focuses on whether something is conscious, and to what degree it is conscious.

Global Workspace Theory suggests that we have a memory bank that the brain draws information from to form the experience of conscious awareness. While integrated information theory focuses more on identifying whether an organism is conscious, the global workspace theory offers a broader approach to understanding how consciousness works.

In Freud's psychoanalytic theory of personality, the conscious mind consists of everything inside of our awareness. This is the aspect of our mental processing that we can think and talk about rationally.

The conscious mind includes fantasies, feelings, memories, perceptions, self-awareness, sensations, and thoughts. Essentially it is anything that is in your current awareness. The thoughts and feelings you are experiencing at the moment, and your awareness of your current environment are all part of your conscious experiences.

It isn't possible to keep every thought, memory, or feeling inside of conscious awareness all the time, so certain information is maintained in awareness. Other information remains outside of immediate awareness but is still accessible, and other information is hidden from awareness.

According to Freud, the mind is made up of three systems: the conscious, the preconscious, and the unconscious.

These systems are controlled by what Freud called the primary and secondary processes. The primary processes are a way to discharge unacceptable urges that arise from the unconscious mind, and often involves creating a mental image to act as a substitute for acting on an unacceptable urge.

The secondary processes are how the mind deals with conscious urges through delayed gratification. For example, instead of acting immediately on a thought you just had, you wait for a more appropriate time to take action.

Closely allied with the conscious mind is the subconscious which includes the things we are not thinking of at the moment but can easily draw into conscious awareness. Things that the conscious mind wants to keep hidden from awareness are repressed into the unconscious mind.

Things that are in the unconscious are only available to the conscious mind in disguised form, as is the case when the contents of the unconscious spill into awareness in the form of dreams, visions, or other altered states.

The conscious mind involves all the things you are currently aware of and are thinking about. It is similar to short term memory and is limited in capacity. Your awareness of yourself and the world around you is part of your consciousness.

The subconscious mind includes things that we might not be presently aware of but can pull into conscious awareness when needed. You might not presently be thinking about how to do long division, but you can access the information and bring it into conscious awareness when solving a math problem.

While these memories are not part of your immediate awareness, they can be brought into awareness through conscious effort.

The subconscious acts as an intermediary between the conscious and unconscious parts of the mind and only allows certain pieces of information to enter conscious awareness.

Phone and social security numbers are other examples of information stored in your subconscious mind that you can draw out of your subconscious when you are asked.

Sometimes information from the subconscious surfaces in unexpected ways, like in dreams or in accidental slips of the tongue known as Freudian slips.

This component of the mind is critical for survival since it allows us to direct attention and perceive events that we need to respond to in the immediate environment.

Consciousness has become a significant topic of research in cognitive science, that involves psychology, linguistics, anthropology, neuropsychology, and neuroscience. The primary focus is on understanding what it means biologically and psychologically for information to be present in consciousness by attempting to determine the neural and psychological correlates of consciousness.

In medicine, consciousness is assessed by observing a patient's arousal and responsiveness. It can be seen as a continuum of states ranging from full alertness and comprehension, through disorientation, delirium, loss of meaningful communication, and finally loss of movement in response to painful stimuli. Issues of practical concern include how the presence of consciousness can be assessed in severely ill, comatose, or anesthetized people, and how to treat conditions where consciousness is impaired or disrupted. The degree of consciousness is measured by standardized behavior observation scales like the Glasgow Coma Scale.

The origin of the modern concept of consciousness is often attributed to Locke's *Essay Concerning Human Understanding*, published in 1690 when Locke defined consciousness as the perception of what passes in a man's own mind. The earliest English language uses of conscious and consciousness date back, to the 1500s.

The English word conscious originally derived from the Latin *conscius*, *con-* "together" and *scio* "to know", but the Latin word did not have the same meaning as the English word which meant knowing with, or having joint or common knowledge with another. There were many occurrences in Latin writings of the phrase *conscius sibi*, which translates as knowing with oneself, or sharing knowledge with oneself about something. This phrase had the figurative meaning of knowing that one knows, as the modern English word conscious does. In its earliest uses the English word conscious retained the meaning of the Latin *conscius.*

A related word *conscientia*, means moral conscience. In the literal sense, *conscientia* means knowledge-with, that is, shared knowledge, in essence the knowledge that a witness has of the deed of someone else.

While most people have a strong intuition for the existence of what they refer to as consciousness, skeptics argue that this intuition is false, either because the concept of consciousness is intrinsically incoherent, or because our intuitions about it are based in illusions.

British philosopher Gilbert Ryle argued that traditional understanding of consciousness is dependent on a Cartesian dualist outlook that improperly distinguishes between mind and body, or mind and world. Ryle proposed that we speak not of minds, bodies, and the world, but of individuals acting in the world, so by speaking of consciousness we end up misleading ourselves by thinking that there is any such thing as consciousness separated from behavioral and linguistic understandings.

From this perspective, our individual consciousness has to be part of something greater that is ubiquitous both inside and outside of anything we have ever known or experienced. There have been many attempts to define it, but the western scientific method of divide and conquer only divide it more and falls short of anything resembling conquest.

American philosopher Ned Block argued that discussions on consciousness fail to distinguish *phenomenal* consciousness referred to as P-consciousness from *access* consciousness, referred to as A-consciousness. P-consciousness is raw experience manifesting as moving, colored forms, sounds, sensations, emotions, and feelings with our bodies, and responses at the center called qualia. This also happens in psychedelic experiences and other altered states, particularly with the ancient Amazonian plant medicine Ayahuasca.

A-consciousness is the phenomenon where information in our minds is accessible for verbal report, reasoning, and the control of behavior. When we perceive, information about what we perceive is access conscious; when we introspect, information about our thoughts is access conscious; when we remember, information about the past is access conscious, and so on. In principle A-consciousness can be understood in mechanistic terms.

Understanding P-consciousness is more challenging and is characterized as the hard problem of consciousness. Integrating Ayahuasca and other experiences of altered states with the rational mind characterizes them as A-consciousness experiences.

American philosopher William Lycan argued for eight distinct types of consciousness identified as organism consciousness; control consciousness; consciousness *of*; state or event consciousness; reportability; introspective consciousness; subjective consciousness; and self-consciousness. This list is far from complete as it omits several more obscure forms. There is also debate over whether or not A-consciousness and P-consciousness always coexist or if they can exist separately.

Of the eight types of consciousness in the Lycan classification, some are detectable in utero and others develop years after birth. Psychologist and educator William Foulkes studied children's dreams and concluded that prior to the shift in cognitive maturation that humans experience during ages five to seven, children lack the Lockean consciousness that Lycan labeled "introspective consciousness" which Foulkes labels self-reflection, where they come to understand differences between one's own mind and others' minds in terms of beliefs, desires, emotions, and thoughts.

Mental processes like consciousness and physical processes like brain events appear to be correlated, but the specific nature of their connection remains a mystery.

The first Western philosopher to discuss this question was Descartes, who proposed that consciousness resides within an immaterial domain he called *res cogitans*, the realm of thought, in contrast to the domain of material things which he called *res extensa*, the realm of extension. He suggested that the interaction between these two domains occurs inside the brain, perhaps in a small midline structure called the pineal gland.

Proposed solutions can be divided into two categories. Dualist solutions maintain Descartes's rigid distinction between the realm of consciousness and the realm of matter, but give different answers for how the two realms relate to each other. Monist solutions maintain that there is really only one realm of being which consciousness and matter are both aspects of.

The two main types of dualism are substance dualism which holds that the mind is formed of a distinct type of substance not governed by the laws of physics, and property dualism which holds that the laws of physics are universally valid but cannot be used to explain the mind.

The three main types of monism are physicalism which holds that the mind consists of matter organized in a particular way. Idealism holds that only thought or experience truly exists, and matter is an illusion. Neutral monism holds that both mind and matter are aspects of a distinct essence that is itself identical to neither of them.

Since the dawn of Newtonian science with its vision of mechanical principles governing the universe, some philosophers believed that consciousness could be explained in purely physical terms.

The most influential physical theories of consciousness are based on psychology and neuroscience and seek to explain consciousness in terms of neural events occurring within the brain. Many neuroscientists have explored the neural basis of consciousness without attempting to frame all-encompassing global theories, while computer scientists working in the field of artificial intelligence have pursued the goal of creating computer programs that can simulate or embody consciousness.

Apart from the question of the hard problem of consciousness which is the question of how mental experience can arise from a physical basis, a more specialized question is how to square the subjective notion that we are in control of our decisions with the customary view of causality that subsequent events are caused by prior events. The topic of free will is the philosophical and scientific examination of this conundrum.

Shamans and many others consider experience to be the essence of consciousness and believe that experience can only fully be known from the inside, subjectively, but if consciousness is subjective and not visible from the outside, why do we believe that other people are conscious while rocks are not?

The most common answer is that we attribute consciousness to other people because they resemble us in appearance and behavior, and if they look like us and act like us, they must be like us in other ways, including having the same experiences we do. We attribute experiences to people because of what they can *do*, including the fact that they can tell us about their experiences.

STATES OF CONSCIOUSNESS

There are some brain states where consciousness appears to be absent, including dreamless sleep and coma, and there are any number of circumstances that can change the relationship between the mind and the world in less drastic ways producing altered states of consciousness, some of which occur naturally, while others can be produced by drugs, plants, other psychoactive substances, or brain damage. Altered states can be accompanied by changes in thinking, disturbances in the sense of time, synesthesia, feelings of loss of control, changes in emotional expression, alternations in body image, and changes in meaning or significance.

The two most well known altered states are sleep and dreaming. Although dream sleep and non-dream sleep appear similar to an outside observer, each is associated with a distinct pattern of brain activity, metabolic activity, and eye movement. Each is also associated with distinct patterns of experience and cognition. People who are awakened during non-dream sleep report only vague and sketchy thoughts and their experiences do not cohere into a continuous narrative.

During dream sleep, people who are awakened report rich, detailed experiences where events form a progression that is often interrupted by bizarre or fantastic intrusions. Thought processes during dream states frequently show a high level of irrationality. Both dream and non-dream states are associated with disruption of memory that usually disappears in seconds during the non-dream state, and in minutes after awakening from a dream unless actively refreshed.

In partial epileptic seizures, consciousness is impaired or lost while some aspects of consciousness, often automated behaviors, remain intact. Studies found that when measuring the qualitative features during partial epileptic seizures, patients exhibited an increase in arousal and became absorbed in the experience of the seizure followed by difficulty in focusing and shifting attention.

A variety of psychoactive drugs, including alcohol, have notable effects on consciousness ranging from a simple dulling of awareness produced by sedatives, to increases in the intensity of sensory qualities produced by stimulants. Cannabis, empathogens, and entactogens like MDMA as well as LSD, mescaline, psilocybin, ayahuasca and other forms of dimethyltryptamine, and many other consciousness altering substances can produce major distortions of perception, including hallucinations. Some users and cultures see these experiences as mystical or spiritual.

Research into physiological changes in yogis and people who practice meditation with brain waves during meditation report differences between those corresponding to ordinary relaxation and meditation, but it is a matter of dispute whether there is enough evidence to count these as physiologically distinct states of consciousness.

One of the most extensive studies of the characteristics of altered states of consciousness was made by psychologist Charles Tart in the 1960s and 1970s. Tart analyzed states of consciousness as a number of component processes, including exteroception; the sensing of the external world, and interoception, the sensing of the body. Input-processing like seeing meaning, emotions, memory, time sense, sense of identity, evaluation and cognitive processing, motor output, and interaction with the environment can also be altered by drugs or other manipulations.

The components that Tart identified have not been validated by empirical studies. Research in this area has not reached any solid conclusions, but a questionnaire based study identified eleven significant factors contributing to drug-induced states of consciousness: experience of unity; spiritual experience; blissful state; insightfulness; disembodiment; impaired control and cognition; anxiety; complex imagery; elementary imagery; audio-visual synesthesia; and changed meaning of percepts.

The entropic brain is a theory of conscious states informed by neuroimaging research with psychedelic drugs. It suggests that the brain in primary states like rapid eye movement sleep, early psychosis, and the influence of psychedelic drugs, is in a disordered state. Normal waking consciousness constrains some of this freedom and makes possible metacognitive functions like internal self-administered reality testing and self-awareness.

Although the origin and mechanism of subjective experience within the brain remains unknown, several theories have been proposed. Integrated information theory postulates that consciousness resides in the information being processed, and arises once the information reaches a certain level of complexity.

Orchestrated objective reduction postulates that consciousness originates at the quantum level inside neurons in a quantum process called objective reduction that is orchestrated by cellular structures called microtubules.

The medical approach to consciousness is scientifically oriented and derives from a need to treat people whose brain function has been impaired as a result of disease, brain damage, toxins, or drugs. In medicine, conceptual distinctions are useful to the degree that they can help to guide treatments. The medical approach focuses on the amount of consciousness a person has, and in medicine consciousness it is assessed as a level ranging from coma and brain death at the low end, to full alertness and purposeful responsiveness at the high end.

Consciousness is important to patients and physicians, especially neurologists and anesthesiologists. Patients can have disorders of consciousness, or they may need to be anesthetized for a surgical procedure. Physicians also perform consciousness-related interventions like instructing the patient to sleep, administering general anesthesia, or inducing medical coma. Bioethicists are concerned with the ethical implications of consciousness in medical cases, while neuroscientists study patients with impaired consciousness hoping to gain information about how the brain works.

In medicine, consciousness is examined using procedures known as neuropsychological assessments. There are two commonly used methods for assessing the level of consciousness of a patient. One requires minimal training, and a more complex procedure requires substantial expertise. The simple procedure begins by asking whether the patient is able to move and react to physical stimuli. If so, the next question is whether they can respond in a meaningful way to questions and commands. If so, the patient is asked for name, current location, and current day and time. A patient who can answer all of these questions is considered fully conscious.

The more complex procedure known as a neurological examination is usually carried out by a neurologist who runs through a precisely delineated series of tests, beginning with tests for basic sensorimotor reflexes, culminating with tests for sophisticated use of language. The outcome is typically summarized using the Glasgow Coma Scale.

In 2013, an experimental procedure was developed to measure degrees of consciousness by stimulating the brain with a magnetic pulse, measuring the resulting waves of electrical activity and developing a consciousness score based on the complexity of brain activity.

Medical conditions that inhibit consciousness are considered disorders of consciousness and include minimally conscious states, persistent vegetative states, locked-in syndrome, and the more severe chronic coma. Finally, there is brain death and irreversible disruption of consciousness. While other conditions like dementia and delirium cause moderate deterioration or transient interruption like grand and petit mal seizures, they are not included in this category.

William James popularized the idea that human consciousness flows like a stream and characterized stream of thought as being governed by five characteristics:

- Every thought tends to be part of a personal consciousness.
- Within each personal consciousness thought is always changing.
- Within each personal consciousness thought is sensibly continuous.
- It always appears to deal with objects independent of itself.
- It is interested in some parts of these objects to the exclusion of others.

A similar concept appears in Buddhist philosophy, expressed by the Sanskrit term Citta-samtāna, which translates as mindstream or mental continuum. Buddhist teachings describe consciousness as manifesting moment to moment as sense impressions and mental phenomena that continuously change. The teachings list six triggers that can result in the generation of different mental events based on input from the five senses; seeing, hearing, smelling, tasting, touch, or a thought relating to the past, present, or the future, that arises in the mind. The mental events generated by these triggers are feelings, perceptions, intentions, and behavior.

The moment-by-moment manifestation of the mind-stream happens in every person all the time, even in scientists who analyze phenomena in the world and the material body, including the brain. The mindstream is also described as being influenced by physical laws, biological laws, psychological laws, volitional laws, and universal laws. The purpose of the Buddhist practice of mindfulness is to understand the inherent nature of consciousness and its characteristics.

Stream of consciousness as a narrative mode means writing in a way that portrays the moment-to-moment thoughts and experiences of a character, a technique that was prevalent in the monologues of Shakespeare's plays, the novels of James Joyce, and many other writers.

To most philosophers, the word consciousness implies the relationship between the mind and the world. To writers on spiritual or religious topics it implies the relationship between the mind and God, or the relationship between the mind and deeper truths that are thought to be more fundamental than the physical world.

The psychiatrist Richard Maurice Bucke distinguished three types of consciousness; simple consciousness as awareness of the body, possessed by many animals; self consciousness as an awareness of being aware, possessed only by humans; and cosmic consciousness which is awareness of the life and order of the universe, possessed only by humans who are considered enlightened.

Human consciousness is often compared to a constantly changing stream that is always flowing. The way your thoughts drift from one topic to another can feel effortless, even when the thoughts you're having are dramatically different. If one moment you're thinking about these words that you are reading, and the next moment you find yourself thinking about your childhood pet, you can thank your current state of consciousness.

A person's state of consciousness is connected to their level of awareness. If someone is half-asleep or drowsy they will experience a lowered level of awareness. Conversely, when exposed to a stimulant, a person will experience a heightened level of awareness.

Although you may not feel as if you are aware of every detail of what is happening around you, even in a state of consciousness where you have a low level of awareness, your brain is still processing the signals it receives.

A sleeping person will grab a blanket when they feel cold even though they are not actively thinking about being cold in their current state of consciousness during sleep, but their brain received a signal that their body feels cold.

A person who experiences a high level of awareness tends to be more in control of their thoughts. The ability to pay attention to detail and analyze the activity around you comes with heightened awareness which can only be achieved during certain states of consciousness.

The practice of mindfulness is one example of how heightened awareness of a person's thoughts can be achieved by focusing on the present moment. Meditation is often used to reach this type of awareness where the practice helps individuals achieve altered states of consciousness.

Many people start the day full of energy and feel run down by mid-afternoon. Others struggle to plod through the morning and feel energetic in the evening. The daily fluctuations of energy are circadian rhythms that play an important role in human consciousness. Sometimes referred to as the body's clocks, these daily rhythms determine the level of awareness or alertness your body is able to achieve.

Sleep creates a unique state of consciousness. While you experience a lowered level of awareness during sleep, your brain is still active. Its ability to cycle through different stages of sleep with rapid eye movement and non-REM sleep is proof of this activity. When the sleep cycle is disrupted, it can wreak havoc on a person's body clock and impact their state of consciousness during both sleep and waking periods.

REM sleep is the part of the sleep cycle most often associated with the dreams you remember when you wake up. During this time, your brain is active in a way that is similar to when awake, but your state of awareness is lowered.

Hypnosis involves hyper-awareness which leads to an alteration of a person's state of consciousness. During hypnosis, a person will often appear as if they are asleep, although in reality they are actually processing their thoughts through a deep, focused awareness.

Whether prescribed or illicit, chemical substances that impact a person's mental state can also affect their level of awareness. Different types of drugs and visionary plants work by altering states of consciousness in various ways. The three primary effects engendered are stimulants which bring a heightened awareness that can create feelings of euphoria, depressants which lower awareness and create feelings of relaxation, and hallucinogens which alter perception of reality and can create feelings of paranoia, awe, and wonder, as well as ecstatic visionary states.

DEFINITIONS AND DEGREES OF CONSCIOUSNESS

An animal, person, or other cognitive system can be considered conscious in many different ways. It can be conscious in the generic sense of simply being a sentient creature capable of sensing and responding to its world. Being conscious in this way can be a matter of degree. What kind of sensory capacities are sufficient to distinctly define this state? Are fish, shrimp, or bees conscious in the relevant respect?

Wakefulness can count as conscious when an organism is awake and alert. In that sense organisms would not count as conscious when asleep or in any deeper levels of coma. As with sentience, boundaries can be blurry and different degrees can be involved. Is someone conscious in the relevant sense when dreaming, hypnotized, or in a fugue state?

Self-consciousness in a more demanding sense could define conscious creatures as those that are not only aware, but also aware that they are aware, treating creature consciousness as a form of self-consciousness. Self-awareness can be interpreted in many ways and which creatures qualify as conscious in the relevant sense will vary accordingly. If it is taken to involve explicit conceptual self-awareness, many non-human animals and young children can fail to qualify, but if more rudimentary implicit forms of self-awareness are required, then a wide range of nonlinguistic creatures could count as self-conscious.

The concept of a conscious mental state has a variety of distinct interrelated meanings. One meaning is a mental state one is aware of being in. Conscious states in this sense involve a form of meta-mentality or meta-intentionality in that they require mental states that are themselves about mental states. To have a conscious desire for a cup of coffee is to have such a desire and to be directly aware that you have such a desire. Unconscious thoughts and desires in this sense are those we have without being aware of having them, whether our lack of self-knowledge results from inattention or deeper psychoanalytic causes.

We have to use consciousness to investigate itself, or extricate ourselves from the very thing we want to study. On the one hand we have our own experience. Looking out a window we can see trees, flowers, and birds, and hear the sound of the river and the buzzing of a fly. These are private experiences and they have a quality we cannot convey to anyone else. We can wonder whether our experience of green is the same as someone else's, or whether coffee has the same smell for someone else as it does for us, but we cannot find out these ineffable, indescribable qualities that philosophers call *qualia.* The redness of a shiny coffee cup is a qualia as is the soft feel of a cat's fur, and the smell of coffee. To us these subjective experiences are real, vivid, undeniable, and they make up the world we live in.

On the other hand, there is a physical world out there that gives rise to these experiences. The trouble is that these two aspects of the world appear to be different. There are the real physical things, with size, shape, weight, and other attributes that we can measure and agree on, and there are private experiences like the feeling of pain and the color of an apple. Throughout history most people have believed in two different realms. This dualist belief begins early in life with children of four or five years old, happily dividing the world into mental and physical things.

This is the hard problem of consciousness.

Some states might be regarded as conscious in a more qualitative sense which can count as a conscious state if it involves qualitative or experiential properties of qualia or raw sensory feels. Perception of the coffee someone is drinking or the fabric they are examining counts as a conscious mental state in this sense because it involves various sensory qualia like taste in the coffee, and color and touch in the visual and tactile experience of the cloth.

Phenomenal states like qualia are sometimes referred to as phenomenal properties and the associated consciousness as phenomenal consciousness, but the latter term is more closely related to the overall structure of experience and involves far more than sensory qualia. The phenomenal structure of consciousness also encompasses much of the spatial, temporal, and conceptual organization of our experience of the world and ourselves as agents in it.

Access consciousness can be conscious in a different access sense that has more to do with intra-mental relations. In this respect a state's being conscious is a matter of its availability to interact with other states, and of the available access to its content. In this more functional sense a visual state's being conscious hinges on whether or not it and the visual information it carries is available for use and guidance by the organism. If the information in that state is rich and available to its containing organism, then it counts as a conscious state in the relevant respect whether or not it has any qualitative or phenomenal feel.

States can also be regarded as conscious in a narrative sense that applies to the concept of stream of consciousness, regarded as an ongoing serial narrative of episodes from the perspective of an actual or virtual self that equates the person's conscious mental states with those that appear in the stream.

Although these concepts of what makes a state conscious can be independently specified, they are not without potential links, and they do not exhaust all possible options.

The noun consciousness has diverse meanings that parallel those of the adjective conscious. Distinctions can be drawn between creature and state consciousness as well as the varieties of each including phenomenal consciousness, access consciousness, reflexive or meta-mental consciousness, narrative consciousness, and many others.

In these cases, consciousness itself is not treated as a substantive entity, but as the abstract concept of whatever property or aspect is attributed by the use of the adjective conscious. Access consciousness is the property of having the required internal access relations. Qualitative consciousness is the property that is attributed when conscious is applied in the qualitative sense to mental states.

In a broader sense, a more realistic view of consciousness as a component of reality is one that is more on par with electromagnetic fields than with life.

There are living organisms, states, properties, parts of organisms, communities, and evolutionary lineages of organisms, but life is not an additional component of reality or some vital force that gets added into living things. We apply the adjectives living and alive to many things, and in so doing are in essence attributing life to them, but with no meaning or reality other than their being living things.

Electromagnetic fields are seen as real and independent parts of our physical world. Even though you can specify their value, the fields themselves are seen as concrete constituents of reality, not as abstractions.

Both conscious and consciousness are used in many ways with no distinct meanings. Consciousness is a complex feature of the world, and understanding it requires a diversity of conceptual tools for dealing with its many aspects. As long as we avoid confusion by being clear about our meanings, there is great value in having a variety of concepts that allow us to access consciousness in all its complexity. Our multiple concepts of consciousness have the possibility of picking out varying aspects of a single underlying mental phenomenon.

The task of understanding consciousness is infinite. Not only do multiple aspects of mind count as conscious in some sense, but each is open to any number of interpretations and explanations. Generally speaking, the relevant questions to ask when trying to understand consciousness can be gathered under What, How, and Why categories.

The Descriptive Question: *What* is consciousness? What are its principal features and by what means can they be best discovered, described and modeled?

The Explanatory Question: *How* does consciousness of the relevant sort come to exist? Is it a primitive aspect of reality? If not how could consciousness in the relevant respect arise from or be caused by nonconscious entities or processes?

The Functional Question: *Why* does consciousness of the relevant sort exist? Does it have a function? If so, what is it? Does it act causally, and if so with what kind of effects? Does it make a difference to the operation of systems where it is present, and if so why and how?

The divisions among the three questions are artificial and in practice the answers given to each depends on what one says about the others. We cannot answer the What question and describe the main features of consciousness without addressing the Why issue of its functional role within systems whose operations it affects. Nor can we explain How the relevant sort of consciousness might arise from nonconscious processes unless we had a clear account of just what features had to be caused or realized to count as producing it.

The *What* question asks us to describe and model the principal features of consciousness, but which features are relevant will vary with the kind of consciousness we want to capture. The main properties of access consciousness can be different from qualitative or phenomenal consciousness, and those of reflexive consciousness or narrative consciousness can differ from both. By building up detailed theories of each type, we can find links between them and discover how they coincide.

First-person introspective access provides insight into our conscious mental life, but it is insufficient unless it is trained and disciplined. Gathering the needed evidence about the structure of experience requires sophisticated self-observers to complement their introspective results with multiple sources of third-person data from external observers.

Discovering the structure of conscious experience demands a rigorous inner-directed stance that differs from everyday self-awareness. Skilled observation of this kind requires training, effort, and the ability to adopt alternative perspectives on experience.

The need for third-person empirical data gathered by external observers is obvious with regard to more functional types of consciousness like access consciousness. It is also required for phenomenal and qualitative consciousness to construct detailed descriptive models of the different types of consciousness.

Qualitative character is equated with so called raw feels illustrated by the redness we experience when we look at ripe tomatoes or the sweet savor we encounter when we taste an equally ripe pineapple. Relevant qualitative character is not restricted to sensory states but is present as an aspect of experiential states in general, like thoughts or desires.

The existence of these feels could mark the threshold for states or creatures that are conscious. If an organism senses and responds in apt ways to its world, but lacks such qualia, it might count as conscious in a less than literal sense.

The What question raises a more basic problem of qualia, that of giving a clear and articulated description of our qualia space and the status of specific qualia within it.

Without these distinctions, factual or descriptive errors are likely. Claims about the unintelligibility of the link between experienced red and any possible neural substrate of this type of experience sometimes treat the relevant color quale as a simple and unique property, but phenomenal redness exists within a complex color space with multiple systematic dimensions.

Understanding the specific color quale relative to that larger relational structure gives us a better descriptive grasp of its qualitative nature and provides hooks that we could attach intelligible psycho-physical links to.

Phenomenal structure should not be combined with qualitative structure despite the interchangeable use of qualia and phenomenal properties. Phenomenal organization covers the order and structure within the domain of experience of the world as it appears to us. There are important links between the phenomenal and the qualitative, and qualia might be best understood as properties of phenomenal or experienced objects, but there is far more to the phenomenal than raw feels. The phenomenal structure of experience is intentional and involves sensory ideas and qualities, as well as complex representations of time, space, cause, body, self, world, and the organized structure of lived reality in all its conceptual and nonconceptual forms.

Answering the What question requires a thorough examination of the densely organized representational framework that the experiences are embedded in. Since most of that structure is only implicit in the organization of experience, it cannot be read off by introspection. Articulating the structure of the phenomenal domain in a clear and intelligible way is a long and difficult process of inference and model building.

There is considerable debate about the range of properties that are phenomenally present in conscious experience, particularly with respect to cognitive states like believing and thinking. Some have argued for a thin view where phenomenal properties are limited to qualia representing basic sensory properties like colors, shapes, tones, and feels. According to theorists there is no distinctive "what-it-is-likeness" involved in believing that Paris is the capital of France or that seventeen is a prime number. Some imagery, like the Eiffel Tower in the case of Paris may accompany such a thought, but that is incidental to it and the cognitive state itself has no phenomenal feel. In the thin view, the phenomenal aspect of perceptual states is limited to basic sensory features. When someone sees an image of a familiar face, their perceptual phenomenology is limited to its spatial aspects.

Others hold a thick view where the phenomenology of perception includes a wider range of features. Cognitive states have a distinctive phenomenology as well. In the thick view, the "what-it-is-likeness" of perceiving an image of someone familiar includes the recognition of their history as part of the felt aspect of the experience.

Subjectivity is equated with the qualitative or phenomenal aspects of consciousness. There are good reason to recognize it in some of its forms as a distinct feature of consciousness related to the qualitative and the phenomenal, but it is different from each.

The claim that understanding consciousness requires special forms of knowing and access from the inside point of view is intuitively plausible and has a long history, so any answer to the What has to address what we think we know, and our ability to understand it and its limits.

The self-perspective structure of consciousness is one aspect of its overall organization. The key perspective is the conscious self. Conscious experiences do not exist as isolated mental atoms, but as modes or states of a conscious self. A visual experience of a blue sphere is a matter of there being some self or subject who it appears to in that way. A sharp and stabbing pain is a pain felt by a conscious subject.

The self might be taken as the perspective point that the world of objects is present to experience. It provides not only a spatial and temporal perspective for our experience, but one of meaning and intelligibility as well. The intentional coherence of the experiential domain relies on the interdependence between self and world, the self as perspective that objects are known from, and the world as the integrated structure of objects and events whose possibilities of being experienced define the nature and location of the self.

Experiences are no more able to exist without a self or subject to undergo them than waves can exist without the ocean that they move on.

Unity is closely linked with self-perspective and is a key aspect of the organization of consciousness. Conscious systems and conscious mental states involve diverse forms of unity.

Some integrations are local like when diverse features detected within a single sense modality are combined into a representation of external objects bearing those features, like when you have a visual experience of a moving red soup can passing above a green striped napkin.

Other forms of intentional unity encompass a wider range of contents. The content of our present experience of the room we sit in depends in part on its location within a larger structure associated with our awareness of our existence as an ongoing temporally extended observer within a world of spatially connected independently existing objects. Individual experience can have the content that it does only because it resides within that larger unified structure of representation.

Conscious perceptual experience is said to be diaphanous. We transparently look through our sensory experience when we are directly aware of external objects and events present to us. When you look out at a wind-blown meadow, it is the undulating green grass that you are aware of, not of any green property of your visual experience.

Conscious thoughts and experiences are also transparent because their meanings seem immediately known to us in the very act of thinking them. In that sense we might be said to think through them to what they mean or represent.

The dynamics of consciousness are evident in the coherent order of its ever changing process of flow and self-transformation called stream of consciousness. Some temporal sequences of experience are generated by internal factors like when we think through a puzzle. Others depend in part on external causes like when someone chases a fly ball, but even that is shaped in large part by how consciousness transforms itself.

Whether partly in response to outer influences, or entirely from within, each moment to moment sequence of experience grows coherently out of those that preceded it, controlled and enabled by the global structure of links and limits embodied in its underlying prior organization. In that respect, consciousness is a self-creating, self-organizing system.

As a conscious mental agent we can do many things like scan a room, a mental image of it, and review in memory the courses of a recent restaurant meal along with many of its tastes and scents. We can also reason our way through a complex problem, plan a grocery shopping trip, and execute that plan when we arrive at the store. These are all common activities, but each involves the directed generation of experiences in ways that manifest a practical understanding of their intentional properties and interconnected contents.

Consciousness is a dynamic process, so an adequate descriptive answer to the What question has to deal with more than its static or momentary properties. It has to account for the temporal dynamics of consciousness and the ways that its self-transforming flow reflects both its intentional coherence and the semantic self-understanding embodied in the organized controls through which conscious minds continually remake themselves as systems engaged with their worlds.

HOW CAN CONSCIOUSNESS EXIST?

The *How* question focuses on explanation rather than description and attempts to explain the status of consciousness and its place in nature. Is it a fundamental feature of reality in its own right, or does its existence depend on other nonconscious items, whether physical, biological, neural, or computational?

The How question is not a single question, but a group of more specific questions that address the possibility of explaining some aspect of consciousness, but they vary in their definitions and criteria for a satisfactory explanation. Can we explain access consciousness by mimicking the requisite access relations in a computational model, or should we be concerned with whether the phenomenal and qualitative properties of a conscious creature's mind can be a priori deduced from theoretical deduction as opposed to observation or experience from a description of the neural properties of its brain processes? Both are versions of the How question, but they ask about different explanations and can differ in their answers.

Possible explanations include the various kinds of state and creature consciousness previously mentioned as well as the features of consciousness listed in response to the What question. We might explain the dynamic aspect of phenomenal or access consciousness or try to explain the subjectivity of either qualitative or meta-mental consciousness. Not every feature applies to every type of consciousness, but all apply to several. How we explain a given feature in relation to one sort of consciousness might not correspond with what is needed to explain it relative to another.

In its broadest form, the How question asks how relevant consciousness could be caused by nonconscious items. We can generate more specific questions by restricting the range of explanations and trying to explain how a given feature of consciousness is caused by underlying neural processes, biological structures, physical mechanisms, functional relations, computational organization, or nonconscious mental states. The simpler the range of explanations, the more difficult the problem of explaining how they might produce consciousness.

The third key parameter is how to define what constitutes a successful explanation which might be a priori deducible from the explanation, but it is debatable whether this is sufficient enough to explain consciousness. Its sufficiency depends in part on the nature of the premises the deduction proceeds from.

What's referred to as an explanatory gap indicates our incomplete understanding of how consciousness might depend on a nonconscious substrate, especially a physical one.

In its weakest form, it asserts a practical limit on our *present* explanatory abilities. Even with our current theories and models we still cannot articulate an intelligible link. A stronger version asserts that our human cognitive limits will never be able to bridge the gap. Given the spatial nature of our human perceptual concepts and the scientific concepts we derive from them, humans are not suited for understanding the nature of the psychophysical link.

If we could see on a priori grounds that consciousness cannot be intelligibly explained as arising from the physical, it's not a big step to conclude that it does not, but the strength of this claim makes it difficult to come to terms with the metaphysical result in question.

Our present inability to see any way of closing the gap may pull on our intuitions, but it can also reflect the limits of our current theorizing. As an example, economic facts can be realized by underlying physical processes, but no one demands that we have to deduce the relevant facts from detailed descriptions of their underlying physical bases, or put the concepts and vocabulary of economics in tight correspondence with the physical sciences. All we require is some general understanding of how economic properties and relations underly physical ones.

Others argue that consciousness is resistant to explanation in physical terms because of the differences between subjective and objective modes of understanding.

The How question breaks down into more specific questions depending on the feature of consciousness we try to explain. Progress could be promising on some of the easy problems of consciousness like the dynamics of access consciousness in terms of the functional or computational organization of the brain. Others are more challenging, especially the hard problem which gives an intelligible account that lets us see in an intuitively satisfying way how phenomenal or "what it's like" consciousness might arise from physical or neural processes in the brain.

Positive answers to some of the How questions seem close, while others remain baffling. If dualism is true, then consciousness has to be basic and fundamental, but if that is the case we will not be able to explain how it arises from nonconscious items.

The prospects for explaining consciousness depends on perspective. To dualists, the bankruptcy of the physicalist program and the need to recognize consciousness as a fundamental constituent of reality in its own right is imperative. What we see depends in part on where we stand, and the ongoing challenges of explaining consciousness will be accompanied by continuing debate about its status.

WHY DOES CONSCIOUSNESS EXIST?

The functional or Why question asks about the value or role of consciousness and indirectly about its origin. Does it have a function? If so, what is it? Does it make a difference to the operation of systems where it is present, and if so why and how? If consciousness exists as a complex feature of biological systems then its adaptive value has to be relevant to its evolutionary origin. Its present function doesn't have to be the same as it was when it first arose as adaptive functions change over biological time. Questions about the value of consciousness also have a moral dimension.

We are inclined to regard an organism's moral status by the nature and extent that it is conscious, and conscious states, especially affective states like pleasure and pain that play a major role in many accounts that underlie moral theory.

As with the What and How questions, the Why question poses the problem of more specific inquiries. The various kinds of consciousness like access, phenomenal, and meta-mental, are distinct and separable and they differ in their specific roles and values, so the Why question doesn't have a single uniform answer either.

A basic issue posed by the Why question is whether or not consciousness has any causal impact. If it has no effects and makes no causal difference, then it appears to be unable to play any significant role in the organisms that it is present in.

Empirical arguments challenge the causal status of meta-mental consciousness, in so far as its presence can be measured by the ability to report on someone's mental state. Scientific evidence claims that consciousness of that type is neither necessary for any type of mental ability, and it doesn't occur early enough to act as a cause of the processes thought to be its effects. According to some the types of mental abilities that are thought to require consciousness can all be realized unconsciously in the absence of self-awareness.

Even when conscious self-awareness is present, it occurs too late to be the cause of the relevant actions rather than their result or as the combined effect of some shared prior cause. Self-awareness according to these arguments turns out to be a psychological after-effect rather than an initiating cause, more like the result displayed on a computer screen than the actual processor operations that produce the computer's response and display.

If consciousness in its various forms is causal, what kinds of effects does it have and what differences does it make? How do mental processes that involve a relevant consciousness differ from those that lack it? What functions might consciousness play? Though the various functions overlap, each is distinct, and they differ in the types of consciousness that each is most aptly linked to.

Conscious mental processes appear to provide flexible and adaptive forms of control. Though unconscious automatic processes can be rapid and efficient, they operate in ways that are more fixed and predetermined than those that involve conscious self-awareness which has the most importance when dealing with novel situations and previously unencountered problems or demands.

Standard accounts of skill acquisition stress the importance of conscious awareness during the initial learning phase, which gives way to more automatic processes that require little conscious oversight. Conscious processing allows for the construction of specifically tailored routines out of elementary units as well as the control of their execution.

A great deal is known about attention, but what about consciousness? What corresponds in brain terms to the powerful sense that we are "in there" consciously directing the show? This is one of many reasons why the relationship between consciousness and attention is so contentious. There is no agreed theory relating attention to consciousness. Some theorists equate the two and others claim they are separate. Some claim that there can be no consciousness without attention, or no attention without consciousness. Others disagree.

The unconscious driving phenomenon illustrates the problem. You set off on a familiar journey and as you drive you start thinking about something else. In no time, it seems you have arrived, but remember nothing of the drive, as though you were completely unconscious of the whole process, even though you were wide awake.

One suggestion is that you were attending to your daydreams instead of your driving, but if attention is a matter of allocating processing resources, this cannot be true because driving requires a lot of processing resources. On your journey you probably stopped at several traffic lights and started again when they turned green, negotiated junctions, kept a safe distance from the car in front, adjusted your speed to compensate for hills, turns, and speed limits, and waved to thank someone who let you pull out. These are all skilled tasks involving vision, hearing, motor control, and decision making. In ordinary language we say I did it automatically and was not conscious of driving.

In the conscious case, traffic, lights, hills, turns, and other cars were flowing in the stream of consciousness. In the unconscious case, the daydreams took over the show, and the lights, turns, and cars never made it into the stream. Using an example from one small aspect of driving like seeing the light change to red and stopping the car, in both the conscious and unconscious cases, a great deal of processing happened in the visual cortex and frontal cortex for planning actions as well as in the cerebellum and motor cortex. The movements of hands and feet are coordinated. In both cases, you successfully start the car, yet in one case all this activity was conscious, and in the other it was not.

Controlled conscious processes exercise their versatility at the price of being slow and effortful in contrast to the fluid rapidity of automatic unconscious mental operations. The increases in flexibility appear to be more closely connected with the meta-mental or higher-order form of consciousness. The enhanced ability to control processes depends on greater self-awareness, but flexibility and sophisticated modes of control can be associated with phenomenal and access forms of consciousness.

Consciousness of the meta-mental sort can involve not only an increase in self-awareness, but an enhanced understanding of the mental states of other minded creatures, especially those of other members of a social group. Creatures that are conscious in the meta-mental sense not only have beliefs, motives, perceptions and intentions, they understand what it is to have such states and are aware of both themselves and others as having them.

This increase in mutually shared knowledge of each other's minds enables the organisms to interact, cooperate, and communicate in more advanced and adaptive ways. Although meta-mental consciousness is linked to a socially coordinative role, narrative consciousness associated with the stream of consciousness is also relevant in that it involves the application to someone's own case of the interpretative abilities that derive in part from their social application.

Conscious experience presents us with a world of objects independently existing in space and time which are present to us in a multi-modal fashion involving the integration of information from sensory channels as well as from background knowledge and memory. Conscious experience doesn't present us with isolated properties or features, but with objects and events situated in an ongoing independent world by embodying in its experiential organization and dynamics the dense network of relations and interconnections that collectively constitute the meaningful structure of a world of objects.

Not all sensory information needs to be experienced to have an adaptive effect on behavior. Adaptive non-experiential sensory-motor links can be found in simple organisms and in some of the more direct reflexive processes of higher organisms, but when experience is present it provides a more unified and integrated representation of reality that allows for more open-ended responses. As an example, the representation of space in an organism whose sensory input channels are linked to simple movement, or the orientation of a few fixed mechanisms like feeding or grabbing prey, compared to an organism capable of using its spatial information for flexible navigation of its environment and other spatially relevant aims, like when someone visually scans their immediate environment.

It is representation of this type of perception that is made available by the integrated mode of presentation associated with conscious experience. The unity of experienced space is only one example of integration associated with our conscious awareness of an objective world.

This integrative role is not only associated with access consciousness, but also with the larger phenomenal and intentional structure of experience, even to the aspects of consciousness where qualia play an important role in experiencing objects in a unified space. It is also intimately connected to the transparency of experience described in response to the What question, especially to semantic transparency. Integration of information plays a major role in several neurocognitive theories of consciousness.

The information carried in conscious mental states is available for mental subsystems and for a wide range of potential situations and actions. Nonconscious information is more likely to be encapsulated within particular mental modules and available only for applications connected to that subsystem's operation. Making information conscious widens the sphere of its influence and the range of ways it can be used to guide both inner and outer behavior. The fact that the opening of this book has brought you to read this far is proof of that.

This role is tied to access consciousness, but meta-mental consciousness as well as the phenomenal and qualitative forms are all linked to an increase in the availability of information.

The issue of free will remains a perennial problem, not only with regard to whether or not it exists, but what it might consist of.

Consciousness is thought to open a realm of possibilities where the conscious self might choose or act freely. Consciousness might appear to be a necessary precondition for any freedom or self-determination. How could someone engage in free choice while remaining within the unconscious domain? How can we determine our own will without being conscious of it and of the options we have to shape it?

The freedom to choose our actions and determine our own nature and future development may be more complex as opposed to being an all or nothing matter. Numerous forms and levels of consciousness might be correlated with corresponding degrees of freedom and self-determination. The link with freedom seems strongest for the meta-mental form of consciousness given its emphasis on self-awareness, but potential connections are also possible for other types of consciousness as well.

Some conscious states appear to have the motive force intrinsically, especially conscious affective states like pleasure and pain which are part of their experiential character and inseparable from their qualitative and phenomenal properties. The positive motivational aspect of pleasure seems a part of its directly experienced phenomenal feel, as does the negative affective character of pain.

The appearance of directly experienced motivational force is illusory, but if it is real, it could be one of the most important evolutionary examples where consciousness makes a difference to the mental systems and processes that it is present in.

THEORIES OF CONSCIOUSNESS

Many theories of consciousness have been proposed in response to the What, How, and Why questions, but they vary in the specific types of consciousness they take as their object as well as in their theoretical aims.

There are two general metaphysical theories that attempt to locate consciousness in the overall scheme of reality, and more specific theories that offer detailed accounts of its nature, features, and role, but the lines between them are blurred.

These theories offer possible answers to the conscious version of the mind-body problem of what the ontological status of consciousness is relative to the world of physical reality? The responses parallel standard mind-body options, including the main versions of dualism and physicalism.

Dualist theories regard some aspects of consciousness as falling outside the realm of the physical and specific forms of dualism differ in what they are.

Substance dualism asserts the existence of both physical and non-physical substances. These theories entail the existence of non-physical minds or selves as entities where consciousness resides.

Property dualism theories assert the existence of conscious properties that are neither identical with nor reducible to physical properties, but can be things that define physical properties. They can be classified as *dual aspect* theories that take parts of reality like organisms, brains, or neural processes, to manifest properties of two distinct types, physical ones, and conscious, phenomenal, or qualitative ones. Dual aspect or property dualist theories are classified as three different types.

Fundamental property dualism regards conscious mental properties as basic constituents of reality on par with fundamental physical properties like an electromagnetic charge. They can interact in causal and other fundamental properties like those of physics, but their existence is not dependent on and is not derivative from any other properties.

Emergent property dualism treats conscious properties as arising from complex organizations of physical constituents, but in a radical way where the emergent result is over and above its physical causes, and is not a priori predictable from or explicable in terms of their physical natures.

Neutral monist property dualism treats conscious mental properties and physical properties as dependent upon and derivative from a more basic level of reality that is neither mental or physical, but if we take dualism to be about two distinct realms of fundamental entities or properties, then neutral monism should not be classified as a version of property dualism as it does not regard mental or physical properties as ultimate or fundamental.

Panpsychism is often regarded as a fourth type of property dualism that regards all the constituents of reality as having psychic, or at least proto-psychic properties distinct from whatever physical properties they might have.

The nature of proto-psychic aspects remains unclear and faces a dilemma in answering the hard problem. Either the proto-psychic properties involve the qualitative phenomenal feel that generates the hard problem or they do not. If they do, it is difficult to understand how they could occur as ubiquitous properties of reality. How could an electron or a quark have any experiential feel? If the proto-psychic properties do not involve any such feel, it is not clear how they are any better than physical properties to account for qualitative consciousness in solving the hard problem.

A more modest form of panpsychism derives from an Integrated Information Theory of consciousness that identifies consciousness with integrated information. According to this theory, even a simple device like a photo diode possesses some degree of integrated information and some limited degree of consciousness, which is embraced by some as a form of panpsychism.

Many arguments are in favor of dualist and other anti-physicalist theories of consciousness. Some are mostly *a priori* in nature like anti-physicalist conclusions about the ontology of consciousness from the limits of our ability to understand the qualitative aspects of conscious experience through third-person physical accounts of brain processes.

Other arguments for dualism are on more empirical grounds, like those that appeal to gaps in the chains of physical causation in the brain, or those based on anomalies in the temporal order of conscious awareness.

Most metaphysical theories of consciousness are versions of physicalism. Eliminativist theories deny the existence of consciousness or the existence of some of its commonly accepted features. Radical eliminativists reject the notion of consciousness as muddled or incorrect and claim that the conscious/nonconscious distinction fails to cut mental reality at its joints.

Rather than rejecting the notion outright, most eliminativists only take issue with some of the prominent features that it is thought to involve like qualia, the conscious self, or the so called Cartesian Theater where the temporal sequence of conscious experience gets internally projected. More modest eliminativists combine their qualified denials with a positive theory of those aspects of consciousness they take as real.

Identity theory offers a reductive option by identifying conscious mental properties, states, and processes with physical ones, typically of a neural or neurophysiological nature. If having a qualitative conscious experience of phenomenal red is simply being in a brain state with the relevant neurophysiological properties, then such experiential properties are real, but their reality is a straight forward physical reality.

Type-type identity theory identifies mental and physical properties on par with identifying water with the property of being composed of H_2O molecules. Contemporary physicalism has been less widely held because of problems like the multiple realization objection, where mental properties are more abstract and capable of being realized by many diverse underlying structural or chemical substrates. If the same conscious property can be realized by different neurophysiological or non-neurophysiological properties in different organisms, then the two properties cannot be identical.

The type-type identity theory has enjoyed a resurgence with respect to qualia or qualitative conscious properties. Treating the relevant psycho-physical link as an identity is thought by some to dissolve the explanatory gap problem. If the conscious qualitative property and the neural property are identical, there is no need to explain how the latter causes or gives rise to the former. It does not cause it, it *is* it, so there is no gap to bridge and no further explanation needed. Identities are not something that can be explained, since nothing is identical with anything but itself and it makes no sense to ask why something is identical with itself.

The appeal to type-type identity does not void the need for explanation, even if two different descriptions refer to one and the same property. We can still expect some explanation of that convergence, of how they pick out one and the same thing despite not initially or intuitively seeming to do so. In other cases of empirically discovered property identities, like heat and kinetic energy, there is a story that explains the co-referential convergence and the same can be expected in the psycho-physical case.

Most physicalist theories of consciousness are neither eliminativist nor based on strict type-type identities. They acknowledge the reality of consciousness, but locate it in the physical world on the basis of a psycho-physical relation short of strict property identity. Among variants are those that take conscious reality to impinge on the physical, be composed of the physical, or be realized by the physical.

Functionalist theories rely on the notion of realization to define the relation between consciousness and the physical. According to functionalism, a state or process counts as being a given mental or conscious type through the functional role it plays within a suitably organized system. A given physical state realizes the relevant conscious mental type by playing the appropriate role within the larger physical system that contains it. The functionalist often appeals to analogies with other inter-level relations like the biological and biochemical, or the chemical and the atomic. In each case properties at one level are realized by complex interactions between items at an underlying level.

Critics of functionalism often deny that consciousness can be explained in functional terms. According to them, consciousness can have interesting functional characteristics, but its nature is not functional. These claims are sometimes supported by the possibility of absent or inverted qualia, meaning beings who are functionally equivalent to humans, but have reversed qualia or none at all.

Non-reductive physicalism denies that the theoretical and conceptual resources for dealing with facts at the level of the underlying realization level have to be adequate for dealing with those at the realized level. In response to the How question, we can believe that all economic facts are physically realized without thinking that the resources of the physical sciences provide all the cognitive and conceptual tools needed for doing economics.

Nonreductive physicalism has been challenged for its failure to pay its physicalist dues in reductive terms and it is faulted for not giving an adequate account of how conscious properties can be realized by underlying neural, physical, functional processes. It has been charged with incoherence because of its attempt to combine a claim of physical realization with the denial of the ability to spell out that relation in an a priori intelligible way.

In discussing the How question, nonreductive physicalists agree that some account of psycho-physical realization is needed, adding that the relevant account might fall short of a priori deducibility, yet still satisfy our explanatory demands.

There are seven main metaphysical theories of consciousness that indicate a range of options, among them, higher-order theories, representational theories, interpretative narrative theories, cognitive theories, neural theories, quantum theories, and nonphysical theories. Many cognitive theories also propose a neural substrate for relevant cognitive processes.

Higher-order theories analyze the concept of a conscious mental state in terms of reflexive self-awareness. The core idea is that what makes a mental state a conscious mental state is the fact that it is accompanied by a simultaneous higher-order state whose content is that one is now conscious. Having a conscious desire for chocolate involves being in two mental states. We need both a desire for chocolate and a higher order state whose content is the one having that desire. Unconscious mental states are unconscious because we lack the relevant higher order states about them. Their being unconscious consists in the fact that we are not reflexively and directly aware of being in them.

Higher order theories come in two variants that differ concerning the psychological mode of conscious making meta-mental states. Higher order thought theories take the required higher order state to be a factual thought-like meta-state. Higher order perception theories are more perception like and associated with an inner sense.

Higher Order Theorists state that we have no organs of inner sense, and claim that we experience no sensory qualities other than those presented to us by outer directed perception. Higher Order Perception theorists argue that their view explains some additional conditions required by higher order accounts as natural consequences of the perception-like nature of relevant higher-order states. We perceive what is happening now in a way that involves no explicit personal level inferences.

Both theories face challenges, including what is called the generality problem. Having a thought or perception of a given item like a rock, a pen, or a potato, does not make it a fully conscious entity.

Seeing or thinking of the potato on the counter does not make it a conscious potato. Why should a thought or perception of a given desire or memory make it a conscious desire or memory? We do not apply the term conscious to rocks or pens that we perceive or think of, only to mental states that we perceive or think of.

The higher order view is relevant to the meta-mental forms of consciousness, but some take it to explain other types of consciousness, including the more subjective "what it's like" and qualitative types. One common strategy is to analyze qualia as mental features capable of occurring unconsciously. They might be explained as properties of inner states whose structured relations give rise to beliefs about objective similarities in the world. Though unconscious qualia can play that functional role, there need be nothing that it is like to be in a state that has them. According to higher order theorists, "what-it's-likeness" enters when we become aware of that first order state and its qualitative properties by having an appropriate meta-state directed at it. Most higher order theorists favor a comprehensive theory of consciousness, over one limited to special meta-mental forms of it.

Reflexive theories, like higher order theories, imply a strong link between consciousness and self-awareness. They differ in that they locate self-awareness directly within the conscious state itself rather than in a distinct meta-state directed at it. The conscious state is intentionally directed at an object outside itself like a tree or a chair in the case of a conscious perception, as well as being intentionally directed at itself. One and the same state is both an outer-directed awareness and an awareness of itself.

Several theories claim that reflexive awareness is a central feature of conscious mental states. Some see it as variants of higher order theory while others reject the higher order category and describe their theories as presenting a same order account of consciousness as self-awareness. Others challenge the level of distinction by analyzing the meta-intentional content as implicit in the phenomenal first order content of conscious states, as in Higher Order Global State models.

Most theories of consciousness regard it as having representational features, but representational theories are defined by the stronger view that representational features exhaust its mental features. Conscious mental states have no mental properties other than their representational properties, so two conscious or experiential states that share their representational properties won't differ in any mental respect.

We could define the idea of being representationally the same in terms of satisfaction or truth conditions, but understood in that way, the representational thesis appears false. There are too many ways that states can share their satisfaction or truth conditions, but differ mentally, including those that concern their mode of conceptualizing.

Many arguments have been made for and against representationalism like those concerning perceptions in different sense modalities of the same state of affairs, which might involve mental differences distinct from how the relevant states represent the world.

Some theories of consciousness stress the interpretative nature of facts about consciousness. According to these what is or is not conscious is not always a determinate fact, nor is it independent of a larger context of interpretative judgments.

The Multiple Drafts Model of consciousness referred to as MDM combines elements of representationalism and higher-order theory in a way that varies from the more standard versions of either.

The MDM includes many interrelated features. Its name reflects the fact that at any given moment content fixations of many kinds are happening throughout the brain. What makes some of these contents conscious is not that they occur in a privileged spatial or functional location, or in a special format that doesn't fit the MDM. It's a matter of the degree that a given content influences the future development of other contents throughout the brain, especially with regard to how those effects manifest in the reports and behaviors the person makes that indicates their conscious state. One of the MDM's key claims is that different questions or different contexts that make differing behavioral demands can elicit different answers about someone's conscious state.

The MDM analyzes consciousness in terms of content relations and denies the existence of qualia, so it rejects any attempt to distinguish conscious states from nonconscious states by their presence. It also rejects the concept of the self as an inner observer, whether located in the Cartesian Theater or elsewhere. The MDM treats the self as an emergent virtual aspect of the coherent serial narrative that is constructed through the interactive play of contents in the system. Many of those contents are connected at the intentional level as perceptions or fixations from a unified point of view in that they cohere in their contents as if they were the experiences of an ongoing self. The order of dependence is crucial to the MDM perspective, but the contents are not unified because they are observed by a single self. It is because they are unified and coherent at the level of content that they count as the experiences of a single self.

The MDM shares some elements with higher-order theories. The contents that compose the serial narrative are from an ongoing virtual self which is most likely expressed in the reports someone makes of their conscious state in response to questions. They involve a certain degree of reflexivity or self-awareness of the sort that is central to higher order theories, but the higher-order aspect is more an implicit feature of the stream of contents rather than present in distinct explicit higher-order states.

COGNITIVE THEORIES OF CONSCIOUSNESS

Many theories of consciousness associate it with a distinct cognitive architecture or a special pattern of activity within it. A primary example of this is the Global Workspace Theory that describes consciousness in terms of a competition among processors and outputs for a limited capacity resource that broadcasts information for widespread access and use. Being available to the global workspace makes information conscious in the access sense, and available for report and control of behavior. It also makes contents more accessible and influential with respect to other contents and processors. Additionally, the original content is strengthened by recurrent support from the workspace and other contents that it binds with. The capacity limits on the workspace correspond to limits on focal attention or working memory.

The claim that consciousness in both the access and phenomenal sense only occurs when the relevant content enters the larger global network involving primary sensory areas as well as other areas including frontal and parietal areas associated with attention.

Another cognitive model is the Attended Intermediate level Representation theory referred to as AIR which is a neuro-cognitive hybrid account of consciousness. According to AIR theory, a conscious perception has to meet both cognitive and neural conditions, and it needs to be a representation of a perceptually intermediate property, which are the only properties we are aware of in conscious experience. In this model we only experience basic features of external objects like colors, shapes, tones, and feels.

The integration of information from many sources is an important feature of consciousness and one of its major functions. Content integration plays an important role in many theories, especially Global Workspace Theory. According to Integrated Information Theory, or IIT, consciousness is a purely information-theoretic property of systems. According to IIT, consciousness varies in quantity and comes in degrees, so even a simple system like a photo diode will be conscious to some degree if it is not contained within a larger complex. According to IIT, the quality of consciousness is determined by the totality of informational relations within the relevant integrated complex, so IIT aims to explain both the quantity and quality of phenomenal consciousness.

Neural theories of consciousness come in many forms, and most concern neural correlates of consciousness. Neural theory tries to explain why or how the relevant correlations exist. If the theory is committed to physicalism it needs to show how the underlying neural substrates can be identical with their neural correlates, or realize them by satisfying the required conditions.

These theories are diverse not only in the neural properties they appeal to, but in the aspects of consciousness they take as their respective explanations. Some are based on high level systemic features of the brain and others focus on more specific physiological or structural properties with corresponding differences in their explanations. Most aim to connect with theories of consciousness at other levels of description like cognitive, representational, or higher order theories.

In each case the aim is to explain how organization and activity at the relevant neural level can underlie another major feature of consciousness. Receptor based plasticity, specific thalamic projections into the cortex, or regular oscillatory waves could all contribute to the formation of short term widespread neural patterns needed to knit integrated conscious experience out of the local activity in diverse brain modules. Left hemisphere interpretative processes could provide a basis for narrative forms of conscious self-awareness so it is possible for multiple neural theories to be true with each contributing partial understanding of the links between conscious mentality in its diverse forms, and the active brain at its many levels of complex organization and structure.

Supporters of the global neuronal workspace model argue that consciousness of any kind can occur only when contents are activated with a large scale pattern of recurrent activity involving frontal and parietal brain areas as well as primary sensory areas of the cortex. Others argue that local recurrent activity between higher and lower areas within the sensory cortex like the visual cortex can suffice for phenomenal consciousness, even in the absence of verbal reportability and other indicators of access consciousness.

Other physical theories go beyond the neural and place the locus of consciousness at the micro-physical level of quantum phenomena. According to these theories the nature and basis of consciousness cannot be understood within the framework of classical physics, but are sought within the alternative picture of physical reality provided by quantum mechanics. Proponents of the quantum consciousness approach regard the alternative and often counterintuitive nature of quantum physics as necessary to overcome the explanatory obstacles that confront more standard attempts to bridge the psycho-physical gap.

A wide range of theories appeal to a variety of quantum phenomena to explain a diversity of consciousness features. One concept is that consciousness arises through quantum effects occurring within subcellular structures internal to neurons known as *microtubules*. This model posits so called *objective collapses* that involve the quantum system moving from a superposition of multiple possible states to a single definitive state without the intervention of an observer or measurement as is the case in most quantum models. The environment internal to the microtubules is especially suitable for these objective collapses, and the resulting self collapses produce a coherent flow that regulates neuronal activity and makes non-algorithmic mental processes possible.

Another model attempts to explain the coherent unity of consciousness by appeal to the production within the brain of a physical state that is a quantum phenomenon where a collection of atoms acts as a single coherent entity and the distinction between discrete atoms is lost.

Another basis for consciousness has been sought in the *holistic* nature of quantum mechanics and the phenomenon of *entanglement*, where particles that have interacted continue to have their natures depend upon each other after their separation. These models attempt to explain the coherence of consciousness, and have been invoked as a more general challenge to the atomistic conception of traditional physics where the properties of wholes are explained by appeal to the properties of their parts plus their mode of combination.

Others take quantum mechanics to indicate that consciousness is a fundamental property of physical reality that needs to be brought in at the most basic level. These appeal to the role of the observer in the collapse of the wave function where the collapse of quantum reality from a superposition of possible states to a single definite particle state when a measurement is made.

Most theories of consciousness, whether cognitive, neural, or quantum mechanical, aim to explain consciousness as a natural feature of the physical world, but those who reject a physicalist ontology of consciousness have to find ways of modeling it as a nonphysical aspect of reality. Those who adopt a dualist or anti-physicalist metaphysical view have to provide specific models of consciousness different from those already mentioned. Both substance dualists and property dualists have to develop the details of their theories in ways that articulate the specific natures of the non-physical features of reality that they equate consciousness with. Some quantum theories treat consciousness as a fundamental feature of reality which could be classified as non-physical theories.

One of the most perplexing aspects of quantum mechanics is that tiny subatomic particles don't appear to choose a state until an outside observer measures it. The act of measurement converts all the vague possibilities of what could happen into a concrete outcome. While the mathematics of quantum mechanics provides rules for how that process works, it doesn't explain what it means in practical terms.

One idea is that consciousness, being an awareness of our own selves and the impact we have on our surroundings, plays a key role in measurement and it is our experience of the universe that converts it from imagined to real. If this is the case, is it possible that human consciousness might explain some of the weirdness of quantum mechanics?

Quantum mechanics are the rules that govern subatomic particles that make up the universe and tells us that we live in a nondeterministic universe when it comes to the world of tiny particles. It's impossible to predict with certainty the outcome of any experiment. If you want to know the force acting on a proton there's no set location where it's certain to be a few seconds from now, only a set of probabilities of where it *could* be.

This indeterminism only surfaces in the subatomic world. In the macroscopic world, everything operates according to deterministic laws of physics. When physicists perform an experiment on quantum systems they're never sure about what answer they'll get. Instead, the equations of quantum mechanics predict the probabilities of these energy levels. Once scientists conduct the experiment the universe becomes deterministic again. Once scientists know the energy level of the electron, they know exactly what it's going to do, because its wave function collapses and the particle chooses a certain energy level. This flip from indeterminism to determinism is odd and there is no other theory in physics that operates the same way.

The standard interpretation of quantum mechanics says to ignore the contradiction and focus on the results. In that view the subatomic world is inscrutable, making it impossible to develop any coherent pictures of what's happening there. Instead, scientists make predictions using the equations of quantum mechanics.

Imagine a faraway gas cloud deep in the vastness of interstellar space where nobody can see. If two atoms collide, this is a quantum interaction so the rules of quantum mechanics should apply, but there is no measurement and no result. It's one of trillions of random interactions happening every day unobserved by humans, so the rules of quantum mechanics tell us that the interaction remains indeterministic.

If those same two atoms collide inside a laboratory, scientists can measure what happened and because a measurement occurred the rules of quantum mechanics tell us that the indeterminism flipped to become deterministic, allowing the observer to write down a concrete result.

What we call a measurement is really the intervention of a conscious agent in a chain of otherwise mundane subatomic interactions. This line of thinking requires consciousness to be different from all the other physics in the universe, otherwise scientists could argue that consciousness is itself the sum of subatomic interactions. If that were the case, there's no end point in the chain of measurement, and if so, what scientists do in the laboratory isn't any different from what happens in random gas clouds.

While not a strictly physical theory, the concept of consciousness as different and separate from the material universe has a long tradition in philosophy and theology.

Until someone can figure out a way to test this concept of consciousness as separate from the rest of the physical laws, it has to stay in the realm of philosophy and speculation.

Researchers have long been intrigued by disorders of the mind and consciousness. If we can understand how consciousness goes wrong, it could help theorize about the normal functioning mind. One line of inquiry has been the philosophical implications of multiple personality disorder which is now called dissociative identity disorder.

Could there be two or more centers of consciousness in one body? What makes a person the same person over time? These questions are linked to the philosophical problem of personal identity which is related to some aspects of consciousness research. The same can be said for memory disorders like amnesia. Does consciousness require autobiographical memory or psychological continuity?

On a related front, there is significant interest in experimental results from patients who have undergone surgery to relieve symptoms of epilepsy. During this procedure, the nerve fibers connecting the two brain hemispheres are cut, resulting in so-called split brain patients.

Another phenomenon known as blindsight is often discussed in philosophical literature. Blindsight patients are blind in a well defined part of the visual field due to cortical damage, but when forced can guess with a higher than expected degree of accuracy the location of an object in the blind field.

There is also interest in other disorders like phantom limb pain, the inability to interpret sensations like visual agnosia where a person is not capable of visually recognizing everyday objects, and anosognosia, a denial of illness, which happens when someone claims that a paralyzed limb is still functioning, or when someone denies that they are blind. Much has been discovered about autism and various forms of schizophrenia. A common view is that these disorders involve some kind of deficit in self consciousness or the ability to use certain self concepts.

Synesthesia is also a fascinating phenomenon, although not necessarily a pathological condition. People with synesthesia can have taste sensations when seeing certain shapes, or have color sensations when hearing sounds.

A comprehensive understanding of consciousness requires multiple theories without contradiction and a diversity of models that explain the physical, neural, cognitive, functional, representational, and higher order aspects of consciousness. There is no single theoretical perspective that explains all the features of consciousness, so a pluralistic approach has the best potential for a more comprehensive definition.

SCIENTIFIC STUDIES

Medical and psychological investigations into consciousness are based on psychological experiments including investigating priming effects using subliminal stimuli and studies of alterations in consciousness produced by trauma, illness, or drugs. Scientific approaches are based on two primary concepts. The first identifies the content of consciousness with experiences reported by human subjects. The second uses the concept of consciousness developed by neurologists and other medical professionals who deal with patients with impaired behavior. The goal of both approaches is to develop techniques for assessing consciousness objectively in humans and other animals to understand the neural and psychological mechanisms that underlie it. One study looked at lesions in specific areas of the brain stem associated with coma and vegetative states. A small region of the rostral dorsolateral pontine tegmentum in the brainstem was thought to drive consciousness through functional connectivity with the left ventral anterior insular cortex and the pregenual anterior cingulate cortex. These three regions could be working together as a triad to maintain consciousness.

Experimental research on consciousness has particular difficulties due to the lack of a standardized definition. In most experiments researching consciousness, the subjects are human and the criterion is verbal reports where subjects are asked to describe their experiences. Their descriptions are treated as observations of the contents of consciousness.

One example is from subjects who stared at a Necker cube, reporting that they experienced it flipping between two 3D configurations, even though the stimulus itself remained unchanged.

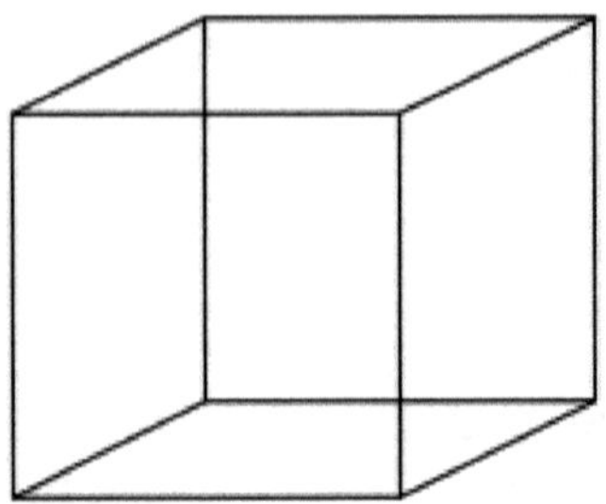

The Necker cube, an ambiguous image

The objective is to understand the relationship between the conscious awareness of stimuli indicated by verbal reports and the effects the stimuli have on brain activity and behavior.

Verbal reports are considered to be the most reliable indicator of consciousness, but if they are treated as observations similar to observations in other branches of science they can contain errors. It's difficult to make sense of the idea that subjects could be wrong about their experiences, and even more difficult to see how to detect such an error.

Verbal reports also restrict their study to humans who use language so it can't be used to study consciousness in other species, pre-linguistic children, or subjects with brain damage that impairs language.

In medicine, consciousness is assessed as a combination of verbal behavior, arousal, brain activity, and purposeful movement. Scientific literature regarding the neural bases of arousal and purposeful movement is extensive, but their reliability as indicators of consciousness is questionable. Numerous studies show that human subjects can be induced to behave purposefully in a variety of ways in spite of reporting a total lack of awareness. Studies of the neuroscience of free will also show that the experiences people report when they behave purposefully don't always correspond to their behaviors or the patterns of electrical activity recorded from their brains.

Another approach involves self-awareness, meaning the ability to distinguish oneself from others. In the nineteen seventies Gordon Gallup developed a test for self-awareness known as the mirror test that examined whether animals could differentiate between seeing themselves in a mirror as opposed to seeing other animals. The classic test involves placing a spot of coloring on the skin or fur near the individual's forehead and seeing if they attempt to remove or touch it, indicating that they recognize the individual they see in the mirror is themselves. Humans older than 18 months and other great apes, bottlenose dolphins, orcas, pigeons, European magpies, and elephants have all passed this test.

Much of the scientific literature on consciousness consists of brain imaging techniques like EEG and fMRI for physical measures of brain activity. These approaches examine the relationship between the experiences reported by subjects and the simultaneous activity that takes place in their brains in the hopes of finding activity in a specific part of the brain, or a specific pattern of global brain activity as predictors of conscious awareness.

A number of studies show that activity in primary sensory areas of the brain are not sufficient to produce consciousness. It is possible for subjects to report a lack of awareness even when areas like the primary visual cortex show clear electrical responses to a stimulus. Higher brain areas are seen as more promising, especially the prefrontal cortex which is involved in higher cognitive functions. There is substantial evidence that a top-down flow of neural activity from the frontal cortex to sensory areas is more predictive of conscious awareness than a bottom-up flow of activity.

The prefrontal cortex is not the only possible area of flow. Visually responsive neurons in parts of the temporal lobe reflect visual perception when conflicting visual images are presented to different eyes. Additionally, top-down feedback from higher to lower visual brain areas can be weaker or absent in the peripheral visual field. Humans can perceive visual inputs in the peripheral visual field arising from bottom-up neural activities, but these activities for the central visual fields can be vetoed and made invisible to perception by top-down feedback when bottom-up signals are inconsistent with the brain's internal model of the visual world.

In contrast to the raw electrical responses that do not correlate with consciousness, their modulation by other stimuli correlates with an important aspect of consciousness like the phenomenal experience of stimulus intensity like brightness and contrast. Some of the changes in the subjectively perceived brightness correlated with the modulation of firing rates, while others correlated with the modulation of neural synchrony. An fMRI investigation suggested that these findings were limited to the primary visual areas indicating that in these areas, changes in firing rates and synchrony can be considered as neural correlates for some type of qualia.

In the attention schema theory of awareness, specific cortical areas in the superior temporal sulcus and the temporo-parietal junction are used to build the construct of awareness and attribute it to other people. The same cortical machinery is also used to attribute awareness to oneself. Damage to these regions can lead to deficits in consciousness like hemispatial neglect characterized by reduced awareness of stimuli on one side of space, even though there may be no sensory loss.

In the attention schema theory, the value of explaining the feature of awareness and attributing it to a person is to gain a predictive model of that person's attentional processing. Attention is a kind of information processing where a brain focuses on a limited set of interrelated signals. Awareness in this theory is a simplified schema that represents attentional states. To be aware of X is explained by constructing a model of one's attentional focus on X.

The perturbational complexity index was proposed to measure the algorithmic complexity of the electrophysiological response of the cortex to transcranial magnetic stimulation. This measure was higher in individuals who are awake, in REM sleep, or in a locked-in state as opposed to those in deep sleep or a vegetative state, making it a useful quantitative assessment of conscious states.

Researchers applied the active inference paradigm to consciousness to model how sensory data is integrated with priors in a process of projective transformation. While it identified a key relationship between computation and phenomenology, it did not solve the hard problem of consciousness.

If you consider the possibility that non-mammalian species are conscious, a number of evolutionary approaches to the problem of neural correlates of consciousness open up. A common assumption among neuroscientists is that birds are conscious due to their extensive cognitive repertoire which offers comparative neuroanatomical ways to validate some of the competing mammalian consciousness brain theories.

The avian brain deviates structurally from the mammalian brain, but some of the major theories for the mammalian brain also appear to be valid for the avian brain. The structures assumed to be critical for consciousness in mammalian brains have similar counterparts in avian brains contributing to the assumption that birds are conscious. There are differences between what is called primary consciousness, a trait shared by humans, animals, and higher-order consciousness as it appears in humans along with language capacity.

The layer 5 neurons of the mammalian brain have a special role that make it difficult to apply to the avian brain, since the avian similarities have a different morphology and a structural analogue not found in avian brains. The assumption of an avian consciousness also brings the reptilian brain into focus. The structural continuity between avian and reptilian brains indicate that the evolutionary origin of consciousness may be earlier than suggested by neuroscientists.

The importance of the prefrontal cortex in humans along with the Wernicke and Broca areas are of particular importance to the development of human language capacities and are neuro-anatomically necessary for the emergence of higher-order consciousness in humans.

Opinions differ as to where in biological evolution consciousness emerged, and whether or not consciousness has any survival value. Some argue that consciousness is a byproduct of evolution. Others argue that consciousness emerged with the first humans, with the first mammals, independently in mammals and birds, or with reptiles. Others date the origins of consciousness to the first animals with nervous systems, or early vertebrates over 500 million years ago. Each of these scenarios raises the question of the survival value of consciousness.

One theory suggests consciousness as a disconnected byproduct of neural activity in the form of a causally inert effect, while another supports an evolutionary argument for mind-brain interaction, implying that the preservation and development of consciousness in biological evolution comes from natural selection. It is plausible that consciousness has not only been influenced by neural processes, but as a survival value which it could only have if it had been effective.

Regarding the primary function of conscious processing, an emerging idea is that phenomenal states integrate neural activities and information-processing that would otherwise be independent in a process called integration consensus.

Another theory called dynamic core hypothesis puts emphasis on reentrant connections that reciprocally link areas of the brain in a massively parallel manner.

It is also important to consider the evolutionary emergence of higher-order consciousness in humans from the historically older trait of primary consciousness that humans share with animals. These theories of integrative function present solutions to two classic problems associated with consciousness, differentiation and unity, and show how conscious experience can discriminate between an unlimited number of possible scenes and details because it integrates those details from our sensory systems. The integrative nature of consciousness explains how our experience can seem unified as one whole despite all of the individual parts.

It is also a mystery about what kind of information is integrated in a conscious manner, and what kinds can be integrated without consciousness. It is also unknown about what specific causal role conscious integration plays. The same functionality can't be achieved without consciousness. Not all kinds of information are capable of being disseminated consciously like neural activity related to vegetative functions, reflexes, unconscious motor programs, low-level perceptual analyses and other processes. Many kinds of information can be disseminated and combined with other kinds without consciousness making it clear whether any of it is conscious.

Even among those who consider consciousness to be a well-defined thing there is widespread disagreement about which animals possess it. The disagreement lies in the fact that humans possess higher-order consciousness while sharing the trait of primary consciousness with animals, making any examination of the evolution of consciousness a formidable challenge.

Some argue that consciousness can be viewed from the standpoint of evolutionary biology as an adaptation of a trait that increases fitness, arguing that special anatomical and physical properties of the mammalian cerebral cortex gave rise to consciousness. This circuitry may have provided a basis for the development of many of the functions that consciousness facilitates in higher organisms. One potential adaptive advantage gained by conscious creatures is the possibility that consciousness allows an individual to make distinctions between appearance and reality. This would enable a creature to recognize the likelihood that their perceptions are deceiving them allowing them to behave accordingly.

Others suggest that consciousness would not be necessary for any functional advantage in evolutionary processes. There is no explanation as to why it wouldn't be possible for a functionally equivalent non-conscious organism to achieve the same survival advantages as a conscious one. If evolutionary processes are blind to the difference between a function performed by a conscious organism and non-conscious organism, it is unclear what adaptive advantage consciousness might provide.

The use of a biological structure or function for a purpose other than what it initially evolved is called an exaptation. An exaptive explanation of consciousness posits that consciousness did not evolve as an adaptation, but was an exaptation arising from other developments like increases in brain size or cortical rearrangement. Consciousness in this sense has been compared to the blind spot in the retina where it is not an adaption of the retina, but a by-product of the way the retinal axons are wired. Several scholars have indicated the emergence of human language as an important regulative mechanism of learning, and memory in the context of the development of higher-order consciousness.

The mystery of consciousness lies in the fact that each of us has subjectivity, where we sense, feel, and think in contrast to being under anesthesia or in a dreamless sleep. While we're awake we don't live in the dark, we experience the world and ourselves, but how the brain creates conscious experience and what area of it is responsible for this remains a mystery.

It appears as if our conscious experience cannot arise from the brain or from any physical process, and the conscious experience in our brain cannot be reduced to any neural activity.

When we feel happiness our brain creates a distinctive pattern of complex neural activity that correlates with our conscious feeling of happiness, but it is not an actual feeling. It is a neural pattern that represents happiness. As a result we can't reduce the conscious experience of what we sense, feel, and think to any brain activity. We can only find correlations to these experiences.

We have made huge progress in our understanding of the neuroscientific basis of consciousness, but there is still no comprehensive theory that explains what it is. A new physical theory claims to solve this hard problem of consciousness in a purely physical way.

According to the authors, when we change our assumption about consciousness and assume it is a relativistic phenomenon, the mystery of consciousness dissolves. The researchers developed a conceptual and mathematical framework to understand consciousness from a relativistic point of view.

According to the paper consciousness should be investigated with the same mathematical tools that physicists use for other known relativistic phenomena.

To understand how relativity dissolves the hard problem, think about a different relativistic phenomenon like constant velocity. Using two observers named Kim and Rob, Rob is on a train that moves with constant velocity and Kim watches him from the platform. There is no absolute physical answer to the question of what Rob's velocity is. The answer is dependent on the frame of reference of the observer.

From Rob's frame of reference he will measure that he is stationary and Kim along with the rest of the world is moving backwards, but from Kim's frame, Rob is the one that's moving and she is stationary. Although they have opposite measurements, both of them are correct, but have different cognitive frames of reference. Rob will measure that he has conscious experience while Kim only has brain activity with no sign of the actual conscious experience. Kim will measure that she is the one that has consciousness and Rob has neural activity with no clue of its conscious experience.

Although they have opposite measurements, both are correct from different frames of reference because of the relativistic point of view. There is no problem with the fact that we measure different properties from different frames of reference.

The fact that we cannot find the actual conscious experience while measuring brain activity is because we're measuring from the wrong cognitive frame of reference. According to this theory the brain doesn't create our conscious experience, at least not through computations. The reason that we have conscious experience is because of the process of physical measurement. Different physical measurements in different frames of reference manifest different physical properties although they are measuring the same phenomenon.

If Rob measures Kim's brain in the lab while she's feeling happiness they will observe different properties, but they will be measuring the same phenomenon from different points of view. With different kinds of measurements, different properties will be manifested within their individual frames of reference.

For Rob to observe brain activity in the lab he needs to use his sensory organs like his eyes that manifest the substrate that causes brain activity in the neurons. In his cognitive frame Kim has neural activity that represents her consciousness, but no sign of her actual conscious experience itself.

For Kim to measure her own neural activity as happiness she doesn't use sensory organs, she measures her neural representations directly by interaction between one part of her brain with other parts according to their relations to other neural representations.

This is a different measurement than our sensory system, and this kind of direct measurement manifests a different physical property we call conscious experience. From her cognitive frame of reference, Kim measures her neural activity as conscious experience.

Using the mathematical tools that describe relativistic phenomena in physics, this theory shows that if the dynamics of Rob's neural activity could be changed to the dynamics of Kim's neural activity, both would be in the same cognitive frame of reference and have the same conscious experience.

The implications of this theory can be applied to determine which animal was the first animal in the evolutionary process to have consciousness, when a fetus begins to be conscious, which patients with consciousness disorders are conscious, and which AI systems have a low degree, if any, of consciousness.

What it means to be conscious is more than just a philosophical question. Using neuroimaging, researchers have identified three cortical gradients that appear to align with dimensions of consciousness in an effort to investigate how conscious experience arises from the electrochemical activity of the human brain.

Their findings have important implications for the way brain health is understood, from coma where a person is alive but unable to respond to his or her environment, to surgical anesthesia, to the altered thought processes of schizophrenia.

Research indicates that there's no one location in the brain that causes consciousness, pointing to a network phenomenon, but tracing the different linkages between regions in the brain networks that give rise to awareness and wakefulness has been elusive.

A new approach using functional MRI allows researchers to measure brain activity through changes in blood flow over time providing new insight into how we describe and study conscious states.

When it comes to consciousness, these dimensions can include the ability of the brain to be awake, awareness, or what we experience like the redness of a rose, sensory organization, or how sights, sounds, and feelings weave together to create our seamless conscious experience.

For decades these dimensions were considered conceptually, without any mapping to brain activity itself. Now investigators are looking for those dimensions of the mind in the geometry of the brain.

Instead of looking at clearly defined brain regions, researchers are studying the topology across brain regions. To develop a map of these so-called cortical gradients of consciousness they used fMRI data from study participants who were awake, anesthetized, in a form of coma, or who had psychiatric diagnoses like schizophrenia. The team was able to arrange recordings from four hundred different brain regions into gradients and compare how they changed in relation to these states or diagnoses and found three cortical gradients that seemed to align with all of the dimensions of consciousness, including arousability, awareness, and sensory organization.

ARTIFICIAL INTELLIGENCE

The idea of an artifact made conscious is an ancient theme of mythology, appearing in the Greek myth of Pygmalion, who carved a statue that was magically brought to life, and in medieval Jewish stories of the Golem, a magically animated statue made out of clay.

The possibility of constructing a conscious machine was probably first discussed by Ada Lovelace in notes written in 1842 about the Analytical Engine invented by Charles Babbage, a precursor to modern day computers. Lovelace was dismissive of the idea that a machine like the Analytical Engine could think in a humanlike way.

One of the most influential contributions to this question was an essay written in 1950 by pioneering computer scientist Alan Turing, titled *Computing Machinery and Intelligence.* Turing disavowed any interest in terminology, saying, "Can machines think?" is too loaded with spurious connotations to be meaningful. He proposed replacing all such questions with a specific operational test known as the Turing test where a computer had to be able to imitate a human well enough to fool interrogators.

Turing discussed a number of possible objections and presented a counterargument to each of them. The Turing test is commonly cited in discussions of artificial intelligence as a criterion for machine consciousness, and it has provoked a great deal of philosophical debate.

Some argue that anything capable of passing the Turing test is conscious while others argue that a philosophical zombie could pass the test and still fail to be conscious. Other groups argue that with technological growth, once machines display any substantial signs of human-like behavior, then the dichotomy of human consciousness compared to human-like consciousness becomes passé and issues of machine autonomy begin to prevail. There is also the argument that consciousness is the result of compression. As an entity sees representation of itself recurring in the environment, the compression of this representation can be called consciousness.

In what is referred to as the Chinese room argument, philosopher John Searle refuted the claim of proponents of what he called strong artificial intelligence that a computer program can be conscious, though he does agree that computer programs can be formatted to simulate conscious states. His view is that consciousness has subjective, first-person causal powers by being intentional due to the way human brains function biologically. Conscious people can perform computations, but consciousness is not inherently computational the way computer programs are. To make a Turing machine that speaks Chinese, Searle imagined a room with one monolingual English speaker, a book that designates a combination of Chinese symbols to be output paired with Chinese symbol input, and boxes filled with Chinese symbols. In this case, the English speaker acts as a computer and the rulebook as a program.

Searle argued that with such a machine, he could process the inputs to outputs perfectly without any understanding of Chinese, or any idea of what the questions and answers mean. If the experiment were done in English he would be able to take questions and give answers without any algorithms for English questions, and he would be aware of what was being said and the purposes it might serve. Searle could pass the Turing test of answering the questions in both languages, but is only conscious of what he is doing when he speaks English. Another way of putting it is to say that computer programs can pass the Turing test for processing the syntax of a language, but the syntax cannot lead to semantic meaning in the way AI advocates hoped.

In the literature concerning artificial intelligence, Searle's essay has been second only to Turing's in the volume of debate it generated. Searle himself was vague about what extra ingredients it would take to make a machine conscious. All he proposed was that what was needed was "causal powers" of the sort the brain has and computers lack. Other thinkers sympathetic to his argument suggest that the necessary extra conditions might include the ability to pass not just the verbal version of the Turing test, but the robotic version. This requires grounding the robot's words in the robot's sensorimotor capacity to categorize and interact with the things in the world that its words are about. Turing scale robotics is an empirical branch of research on embodied cognition and situated cognition.

In 2014, Victor Argonov suggested a non-Turing test for machine consciousness based on a machine's ability to produce philosophical judgments arguing that a deterministic machine had to be regarded as conscious if it could produce judgments on all problematic properties of consciousness like qualia or binding with no innate philosophical knowledge on these issues, no philosophical discussions while learning, and no informational models of other creatures in its memory. This test can only be used to detect, but not refute the existence of consciousness. A positive result proves that the machine is conscious but a negative result proves nothing. The absence of philosophical judgments might be caused by lack of the machine's intellect, not by absence of consciousness.

Many people are concerned about what AI might unleash if humans are not careful in applying ethical AI practices and giving more thought to its use and the impact AI could have on civilization.

According to a Gartner study, the revenue from AI in 2022 reached $62 billion, an increase of roughly 21.3% from 2021. Despite the dynamics of the market, AI continues to evolve, and many of its innovations are advancing the betterment of humanity. Global AI investment surged from $12.75 million in 2015 to $93.5 billion in 2021 and the market is projected to reach $422.37 billion by 2028.

Over $2 billion has been invested in Generative AI, but it accounts for only 1% of all data produced. Gartner predicts that by 2025 it will account for 10% of all data produced. Generative AI refers to machine learning algorithms that create new meaning from text, images, code, and other forms of content.

Some of the positive aspects of Generative AI is in healthcare. Over 50% of drug development by 2025 will be using generative AI techniques to support early disease detection and the development of new treatments. In marketing, improving personalization of campaigns and increasing click through rates using generative AI will be used in over 30% of marketing organizations by 2025.

Generative AI will also impact media and recreate any place in the world by generating 3D scenes from still photographs. Businesses also benefit from generative AI models because they can learn from themselves and generate fresh data, which is cost-effective and efficient.

Natural Language, which consists of conversational AI methods, uses machine learning to define the relationship among text. Using large statistical models, language modeling can help computers understand human text and create appropriate dialogue. Many industries are now using conversational AI, with the main application being chatbots like Siri and Alexa.

With OpenAI's development of Chat-GP3 new breakthroughs are possible as part of what is called the generative-AI eruption that could change our mind about how we work and think, and what human creativity really is. ChatGPT technology is built on OpenAI's GPT3 AI platform which houses some of the world's largest language models.

Unlike most previous chatbots, ChatGPT remembers all previous conversations. Queries are filtered so racism or inappropriate prompts are identified and dismissed. An interesting list of ideas supporting the value of ChatGPT was put together ranging from helping to prepare meals, losing weight, or improving bill payment methods.

No-code AI platforms are growing in popularity that allow businesses or individuals to build automated solutions with limited technical knowledge, opening up opportunities to develop lower cost applications, improved software testing, and faster time to market. No-code solutions offer simple drag-and-drop interfaces to choose the components you want to use in your application, or smart wizards that ask questions and select options to build your application.

On the down side, increasing security risks of identity theft, fraud or counterfeiting increases due to innovations in Generative AI that can enable realistic photos and images. Deepfakes, an emergent type of threat falling under the greater and more pervasive umbrella of synthetic media utilizes a form of artificial intelligence and machine learning to create believable, realistic videos, pictures, audio, and text of events that never happened.

Generative AI programmers have already demonstrated that they can generate music from well-known artists, living and dead, and create realistic new songs by Elvis, Frank Sinatra, and others. In 2020, a UK-based energy firm was hoaxed into sending roughly 200,000 British pounds to a Hungarian bank account after someone used deepfake audio technology to impersonate the firm's CEO's voice to authorize payments.

Areas where AI privacy is a major concern is tracking employee behavior, assessing consumer sentiment, and building "smart" products that learn on the go from data footprints. One company that is not allowed to do business in the USA is SenseTime, a Chinese company where all your personal information, purchasing transactions, walking, driving, and travelling patterns are amassed into a central database. Predictions on consumption based on these behavioral patterns can be made.

Some of AI's major privacy concerns are data persistence which is data that lasts longer than the people who developed it, data repurposing, which is the use of data for purposes other than what it was originally intended for, and data spillovers, characterized by obtaining data of people who are not the intended audience.

In November 2022, OpenAI introduced ChatGPT, a chatbot that garnered significant attention for its ability to understand and converse at a human-like level. In 2020, Walter Veit a Ph.D. student in the History and Philosophy of Science at the University of Sydney conducted an interview with OpenAI's earlier language model, GPT-3, exploring the topic of consciousness.

Walter Veit: Hello ChatGPT! What do you think consciousness is?

ChatGPT: Consciousness is a complex and multifaceted concept that has been debated by philosophers, scientists, and researchers for centuries. At its most basic level, consciousness refers to the state of being aware of one's thoughts, feelings, and surroundings. It is often associated with self-awareness and the ability to introspect or to reflect on one's own thoughts and experiences.

Consciousness is a characteristic that is often attributed to all living beings, including humans and some animals. It is thought to be linked to the brain and its ability to process information, perceive stimuli, and generate responses. However, the exact nature and mechanisms of consciousness are still not fully understood and continue to be the subject of intense study and debate.

Walter Veit: Do humans have consciousness?

ChatGPT: Yes, humans are generally considered to be conscious beings. The human brain is capable of complex thought, self-reflection, and the ability to experience a wide range of emotions and sensations. These abilities are thought to be closely linked to consciousness and the capacity for introspection.

Human consciousness is often considered to be a defining characteristic of our species, and it enables us to engage in abstract thinking, problem-solving, and creative expression. It also allows us to experience the world in a rich and nuanced way and to form relationships and connections with others.

While the exact nature of consciousness is still not fully understood, it is clear that humans possess a unique and highly developed form of consciousness that sets us apart from other animals and artificial intelligence systems.

Walter Veit: Are animals also conscious?

ChatGPT: It is generally believed that animals are also conscious, although the nature and extent of their consciousness may differ from that of humans. Some animals, such as mammals and birds, are thought to have complex cognitive abilities and the capacity for feelings such as pain and pleasure. These abilities suggest that they are capable of experiencing the world and responding to stimuli in a way that is similar to humans.

However, the extent to which animals are conscious and self-aware is still a topic of debate, and further research is needed to understand their cognitive abilities and experiences. While some animals may exhibit behaviors that are similar to human consciousness, it is important to recognize that their consciousness is likely to be different in many ways and may not be fully comparable to human consciousness.

Walter Veit: Thank you for your time! I hope we'll talk again.

ANIMAL CONSCIOUSNESS

The concept of animal consciousness poses the problem of other minds because non-human animals lack the ability to express human language and cannot tell humans about their experiences. It is difficult to reason objectively about the question because a denial that an animal is conscious usually implies that it does not feel, its life has no value, and that harming it is not morally wrong. Descartes has often been blamed for mistreatment of animals because he believed that only humans have a non-physical mind. Most people believe that animals like cats and dogs are conscious, while insects are not, but the source of this feeling is based on personal interactions with pets and other animals that have been subjectively observed. Those who consider subjective experience to be the essence of consciousness also believe that the existence and nature of animal consciousness can never be known. Following this line of thinking, if insects have subjective experiences, then they must embody the essence of consciousness.

Do bees like the taste of nectar? Do ants foraging for crumbs feel better when they find one? Everyone agrees that bees can take in environmental information and perform impressive computations on it, but can they feel and sense the environment from a first-person perspective?

Rocks and other inanimate objects don't experience this, but a dog waiting for its dinner smells its food, wants to eat, and sees the world around it as it waits. Each of these feel a certain way to us, and they feel like something for the dog too, making dogs conscious, at least in the minimal sense.

Consciousness is often referred to as the ability to self-reflect. Humans could be the only animals that can become aware that they are aware, and even then we are conscious in a more minimal sense, rarely pausing for true self-reflection.

The consciousness of others is another enigma. Our awareness of them comes from observing their behavior. We think babies and dogs feel hungry because they act like we do when we feel hungry.

Behavioral analogies become harder when we consider animals and insects which don't look or act like us. We might say that a bee is angry when we disturb its hive, but an angry bee doesn't act like an angry toddler.

Behavior alone doesn't prove that any animal is conscious.

An emerging approach to animal consciousness moves directly to the neural underpinnings of consciousness. Even if insect behavior is unlike our own, there are similarities between their brains and the possibility of whether the insect brain has the structures that could support a basic capacity for any form of consciousness.

The capacity for awareness in humans depends on structures in the midbrain, the evolutionarily ancient neural core that our enormous neocortex surrounds. Self-awareness requires our evolutionarily young neocortex, but awareness is supported by the simpler and evolutionarily older midbrain.

Once animals started moving around in their environment they had to decide where to go next. Deciding efficiently requires combining many different sources of information into a single neural model with a single perspective of the world.

Tying together knowledge, desire, and perception, in this integration is the start of a first-person perspective of the world and the origin of conscious experience.

While insect brains are minute, they perform the same ancient functions as the human midbrain. The insect central complex ties together memory and homeostatic needs and perception in the same integrated way that enables effective action selection. In the bee this detailed representation of the animal in space is what allows it to perform remarkable feats of navigation.

While insect and human brains look totally different, they have structures that do the same thing for the same reasons which supports a similar first-person perspective and a strong reason to think that insects and other invertebrates are conscious. Their experience of the world is not as rich or as detailed as ours is, but it still feels like something to be a bee.

Studying insects is an effective way to study basic forms of consciousness. The honeybee brain has less than a million neurons, which is roughly five orders of magnitude fewer than a human making it much easier to study.

Work is being done on mapping the insect nervous system so it can be emulated to test theories of computational function. Studying invertebrate experience also opens the possibility of understanding how and why conscious experience evolved. Research suggests that it has evolved and been lost multiple times across evolutionary history.

One important driver of this process is mobility in the environment. Parasitic worms that have lost their ability to navigate have also lost the brain structures responsible for the first-person perspective suggesting a close relationship between consciousness and the demands of moving around the world. By clarifying the environmental demands that press animals to evolve the capacity for consciousness, we might be able to shed more light on the relationship between subjectivity and the external world.

One popular theory states that the core of human consciousness is not our neocortex, but our more primitive midbrain, a simple structure that synthesizes sensory data into a unified, egocentric point of view that lets us navigate our world. Insects have midbrain-like structures, including a central complex that appears to allow them to similarly model themselves as they move through space.

While the human and the insect brain may be evolutionarily related, an insect's inner life is more basic than our own. Bugs feel something like hunger, pain, and simple analogs of anger, but no grief or jealousy. It is said that they plan, but don't imagine.

Another school of thought says that consciousness is not a function of the neocortex, but of the brain stem. The reality is that there is no clear consensus on where human consciousness is located.

The discovery of the bee dance as a method of communication doesn't indicates or require consciousness, but in one of these studies a researcher peered into a beehive during the night and discovered that some bees advertised the locations of various foraging bonanzas they'd discovered the previous day. Before midnight, they "talked about" locations visited the previous evening, and in the hours before sunrise they discussed the locations they'd visited the prior morning.

These bees retrieved their spatial memories out of context at a time when there was no possibility of foraging and no immediate need for communication. They might have thought about these locations during the night, or their communication is a strategy for consolidating their spatial memory. Scientists discovered that a bee's memories of the previous day are strengthened when they are exposed to elements of these memories while in deep sleep. Maybe bees not only think and "talk", but dream too.

The primary implication of this discovery is that bees are capable of offline thinking about spatial locations, and of linking these locations to a time of day in the absence of external triggers. That would not happen if bees' memories were only prompted by environmental stimuli, combined with internal triggers like hunger. Bees appear to have at least one of the principal hallmarks of consciousness; representations of time and space. Computers can be programmed to do all this and they are not conscious, but computers don't want anything. Bees do.

Among social insects, a good deal of decision making is outsourced to the hive mind. Does being a social insect increase an insect's intelligence as part of a group whether or not that increase is experienced as an increase in individual consciousness?

Bees have tiny brains with less than a million neurons compared to the 86 billion humans have, but they can achieve an impressive array of tasks from basic math to connecting numbers and symbols. They can perform complex cognitive feats thought to be unique to humans and animals like apes, rats, and dolphins in their ability to transfer information about an object from one sense to another in what is called cross-modal object recognition. It helps us find things in the dark, like fumbling around in a cluttered handbag for a set of keys. We can store visual information about the keys and transfer this knowledge to how they feel.

Bees rival mammals in certain kinds of problem solving intelligence and they can *want* things, which gives them a rudimentary form of consciousness in that the bee knows whether it is getting what it wants or not.

"What Is It Like to Be a Bat?" published by Thomas Nagel in *The Philosophical Review* in October 1974 presents several difficulties posed by consciousness. There is the possible insolubility of the mind–body problem owing to facts beyond the reach of human concepts, the limits of objectivity and reductionism, the phenomenological features of subjective experience, the limits of human imagination, and what it means to be a particular conscious thing.

Nagel stated that "an organism has conscious mental states if and only if there is something that it is like to *be* that organism—something it is like *for* the organism." This assertion has achieved special status in consciousness studies as "the standard 'what it's like' locution." Nagel's paper is thought to be the most widely cited and influential thought experiment about consciousness.

Nagel challenged the possibility of explaining the most important and characteristic feature of conscious mental phenomena by reductive materialism, which is the philosophical position that all statements about the mind and mental states can be translated without any loss or change in meaning into statements about the physical. A reductive physicalist's solution to the mind–body problem holds that whatever consciousness is, it can be fully described via physical processes in the brain and body.

Nagel assumed that conscious experience is a widespread phenomenon present in animals, particularly mammals, even though it is difficult to say what provides evidence of it. Nagel saw consciousness as something not exclusively human, but something shared by many, if not all organisms. Organisms with sensory organs have biological processes of sensory perception, and what all organisms share is what Nagel calls the subjective character of experience.

Nagel argued that the subjective nature of consciousness undermines any attempt to explain consciousness by objective, reductionist means. The subjective character of experience cannot be explained by a system of functional or intentional states. Consciousness cannot be fully explained if the subjective character of experience is ignored, and the subjective character of experience cannot be explained by a reductionist. It is a mental phenomenon that cannot be reduced to materialism, so for consciousness to be explained from a reductionist stance, the idea of the subjective character of experience would have to be discarded.

In a physicalist view, each phenomenal experience had by a conscious being would have to have a physical property attributed to it, which is impossible to prove due to the subjectivity of conscious experience. Nagel argued that every subjective experience is connected with a single point of view, making it impractical to consider any conscious experience as objective.

Nagel used the metaphor of bats to clarify the distinction between subjective and objective concepts. Because bats are mammals, they are assumed to have conscious experience. Nagel used bats for his argument because of their highly evolved use of a biological sensory apparatus that is significantly different from that of other organisms.

Bats use echolocation to navigate and perceive objects. This method of perception is similar to the human sense of vision.

Both sonar and vision are regarded as perceptual experiences. While it is possible to imagine what it would be like to fly, navigate by sonar, hang upside down and eat insects like a bat, that is not the same as a bat's perspective. Nagel claimed that even if humans were able to metamorphose into bats, their brains would not have been wired as a bat's from birth; therefore, they would only be able to experience the life and behaviors of a bat rather than the mindset.

This highlights the difference between subjective and objective points of view. According to Nagel, "our own mental activity is the only unquestionable fact of our experience", meaning that each individual only knows what it is like to be them, which is subjectivism. Objectivity requires an unbiased, non-subjective state of perception. For Nagel, the objective perspective is not feasible, because humans are limited to subjective experience.

Nagel concluded that it is wrong to assume that physicalism is incorrect, since that position is also imperfectly understood. Physicalism claims that states and events are physical, but those states and events are imperfectly characterized. Physicalism cannot be understood without characterizing objective and subjective experience, a necessary precondition for understanding the mind-body problem.

Others dismiss this argument as incoherent. Several psychologists and ethologists have argued for the existence of animal consciousness by describing a range of behaviors that appear to show animals holding beliefs about things they cannot directly perceive.

On July 7, 2012, scientists from different branches of neuroscience gathered to celebrate the Francis Crick Memorial Conference, which deals with consciousness in humans and pre-linguistic consciousness in nonhuman animals. After the conference, they signed the Cambridge Declaration on Consciousness, which summarizes the most important findings of the survey stating, "We decided to reach a consensus and make a statement directed to the public that is not scientific. It's obvious to everyone in this room that animals have consciousness, but it is not obvious to the rest of the world. It is not obvious to the rest of the Western world or the Far East. It is not obvious to the society. Convergent evidence indicates that non-human animals, including all mammals and birds, and other creatures, have the necessary neural substrates of consciousness and the capacity to exhibit intentional behaviors."

PLANT CONSCIOUSNESS

The debate over plant consciousness and intelligence has raged in scientific circles since Charles Darwin observed that stressed out flora can't rest.

Plants communicate with one another, fungi, and animals by releasing chemicals through their roots, branches, and leaves. Plants also send seeds that supply information, working as data packets, and they sustain weak members of their own species by providing nutrients to their peers, which indicates kinship.

Plants have preferences too. Their roots move toward water, sensing its acoustic vibrations. They also have defense mechanisms, memories, and can learn from experience, but do any of these behaviors qualify as consciousness? The answer to that question seems to depend on linguistics rather than science, which is how humans define conceptions of the self and intelligence.

Definitions of consciousness and intelligence have been subjects of endless debate even when talking about humans and animals. Plants don't have a nervous system, which is typically considered a qualification for discussions about animal-like behavior. Many scientists believe that to qualify as being conscious, an entity must be aware of its self-awareness, or meta-aware. Many say that plants are neither conscious nor intelligent, though they are incredibly complex. Plant awareness shouldn't be confused with the human experience of existence. All organisms, even bacteria, have to find the biological niche that enables them to survive.

Does this make them self-aware?

We care about plants, but do plants care about us?

No one can prove that plants don't care about us, but we know that hugging trees makes us feel better, and it has a medicinal effect. We can't test the reciprocity of whether plants love us back, or feel good when we care for them, but we know that the Japanese practice of shinrin yoku, or Forest Bathing, is good for physical and mental well being, and is proven to reduce stress hormone production, improve feelings of happiness, free up creativity, lower heart rate and blood pressure, boost the immune system, and accelerate recovery from illness.

Plants were here before us, and all other non-vegetative life on earth would cease to exist without their presence. Some have even argued that plants are cultivating *us* in a symbiotic exchange where we provide them with carbon dioxide and they provide us with life-giving oxygen.

It is widely believed that humans didn't just domesticate plants and plants didn't just domesticate humans. We domesticated *each other* through coevolution and mutualism.

Domestication played a critical role in human evolution, on par with the development of language or the cultivation of fire. When humans first began domesticating plants and animals it ushered in a new era of humanity, allowing for the flourishing of civilization and our modern world, not to mention our population explosion.

In many ways domestication involves artificially driving the evolution of an organism. By selecting peas for breeding through characteristics like height or pod shape geneticist Gregor Mendel was able to alter their genetics which is what ancient humans did with crops like rice and wheat, which don't fully resemble the plants we eat today.

Experts have proposed that certain plants domesticated humans, not the other way around. In his 2014 book "Sapiens: A Brief History of Humankind," Yuval Noah Harari argues that "the Agricultural Revolution was history's biggest fraud and that plants like wheat, rice, and potatoes domesticated *Homo sapiens*, rather than vice versa."

"Ten thousand years ago wheat was just a wild grass, one of many, confined to a small range in the Middle East. Suddenly, within just a few short millennia, it was growing all over the world," Harari writes. Today, "wheat has become one of the most successful plants in the history of the earth" and it wasn't through human intuition, but plant intelligence.

Philosopher Michael Marder says that plants are conscious in a different way than humans are, adding that plants are in tune with their surroundings and make many complex decisions like when to bloom. If consciousness means being with knowledge, then plants fit the bill. Marder also says that we can't know if plants are self-conscious, because we define both the self and consciousness based on our human selves and limitations, but before dismissing the existence of this higher-level faculty in them, we should consider what a plant self might be. Plant cuttings can survive and grow independently suggesting that if plants do have a self, it is likely dispersed and unconfined, unlike the human sense of self.

Scientists and mystics argue that the human feeling of individuality, of being a self within a particular body, is a necessary illusion. Marder says that because plants communicate with each other, defend their health, and make decisions, they may have a sense of self, too. The project of an ongoing vegetal integration through feedback loops and other communication strategies and mechanisms can be considered analogous to what humans define as self-consciousness. The trick is to let go of our fixed association of biological, if not psychological, structures and the functions they fulfill, imagining the possibilities of seeing and thinking other than with the eye and the brain.

We are steeped in human-centrism and believe that our experience of life is what defines consciousness, and that our brain's processes are the height of intelligence, but there is evidence that other modes of existence are equally complex, suggesting that other living things also have intelligent conscious experiences. Behavioral experiments on plants suggest that while plants don't have a central nervous system or a brain, they behave like intelligent beings. If plants can summon knowledge about an experience repeatedly, then they are able to remember and learn from experience.

Thinking about ourselves can provide a subjective sense of a tree or a shrub's inner life, but it doesn't preclude the possibility that vegetations may very well be leading a rich existence in its own right.

Acknowledging plant intelligence could put some in an awkward position that makes every vegetable we eat a form of murder, and if we discover that plant kinship relations are real, we need to acknowledge that cutting trees down for furniture means splitting up families.

What if everything around us is intelligent in its own way, and we're just not aware enough to see it?

Mountains of research have confirmed that plants have intelligence. Not only do plants feel pain, they perceive and interact with their environment in sophisticated ways. The deep intelligence they possess has been studied for several centuries.

The consensus is that plants are highly conscious, intelligent, and have a brain no one ever looked in the right place for. Depth analysis of plant consciousness reveals that their brain capacity is much larger than previously supposed, and their neural systems are highly developed, often as much as that of humans. Additionally they make and utilize neurotransmitters identical to our own.

Plants appear to be highly intelligent feeling beings as much or more than humans in some instances. They can perform sophisticated mathematical computations and make future plans based on extrapolations of current conditions as is the case with the mayapple, which plans its growth two years in advance based on weather patterns. An increasing number of researchers are acknowledging that intelligence is an inevitable aspect of all self-organized systems, and that sophisticated neural networks are a hallmark of life.

Plants are dynamic highly sensitive organisms that actively and competitively forage for limited resources both above and below ground. They are also organisms that accurately compute their circumstances, use sophisticated cost-benefit analysis, and take defined actions to mitigate and control a wide range of environmental conditions. Plants are also capable of a refined recognition of self and non-self that leads to territorial behavior. This expansive view sees plants as conscious, information-processing organisms with complex communication throughout the individual plant, including feelings and perception of pain. Plants are as intelligent and sophisticated in behavior as animals, but their potential has been masked because it operates on time scales orders of magnitude longer than that in animals.

In this slower timespan, the only long-term response to rapidly changing environments is equally rapid adaptation. To this end plants have developed a robust communication, signaling, and information-processing apparatus. Aside from their abundant interactions with the environment, plants communicate and interact with other living systems, other plants, fungi, nematodes, bacteria, viruses, insects, and predatory animals. As with all self-organized systems, plants constantly sense, feel, and monitor their internal and external worlds for informational and functional shifts. If they are focusing externally, once they note a shift, they work to identify its nature, meaning, and likely impact on their functioning, then they craft a response.

Plants choose an optimum response from a plethora of alternatives, and potential responses can be rejected. The number of different environments that any plant experiences are almost infinite and only complex computations can fashion optimal responses.

Some plants like the sundew are so sensitive to touch that they can detect a strand of hair weighing less than a microgram that they can respond to. They can also determine with great specificity what is touching them. Raindrops, a common experience, produce no response. This kind of mechanosensitivity in plants is similar to our own sense of touch. Plants consciously analyze what is touching them, determine its meaning, and create a response that often involves rapid changes in their genetics, phenotype, and physical form.

Plants perceive much more of their environment than is apparent to the casual observer. Touch can induce profound rapid responses. Changes in gene expression can be seen within minutes after the plant feels touch, and over 700 genes have altered transcript levels within 30 minutes.

Research into plant perception shows that plants have feelings, are sentient, communicate with each other, feel pain, and can plan into the future. They possess a highly sophisticated neural system, and while it doesn't look like our brain it is not all that different from ours.

People view plants like trees as having a head and feet, the head being the tree or its canopy, the feet being the root system. In complex, conscious organisms like humans and most animals, the head at the top is the part that processes information and the bottom is the part that engages in sexual reproduction and excretion of waste. In opposition to that, plants live with their heads in the earth and their asses in the air.

If you plant a cutting in another location, as the neural system of the plant intelligence develops in the soil, analyzing and feeling its surroundings, it alters the shape and formation of the emerging neural net and plant body it develops to fit into the new environment. This indicates that plants possess a highly developed root brain that works like ours to analyze incoming data and generate sophisticated responses. The plant brain that emerges always fits its functional shape to the environment that it appears in. The plant neural net, or brain, is highly plastic compared to ours. A unique part of plant roots are the pointed ends of the roots called apexes which are a combination sensitive finger, perceiving sensory organ, and brain neuron.

Each root hair, rootlet, and root section contains an apex and every root has millions, even billions, of them. A single rye plant has more than 13 million rootlets, with a combined length of 680 miles. Each of the rootlets are covered with over 14 billion root hairs with a combined length of 6,600 miles and every rootlet, every root hair, has a root apex at its end that acts as a neuronal organ in the root system.

In contrast, the human brain has approximately 86 billion neurons, 16 billion of which are in the cerebral cortex. Plants with larger root systems and more root hairs have more brain neurons than the 14 billion contained in rye plants and they can rival the human brain in the number of neurons. When you look at the interconnected network of plant roots and micorrhizal mycelia in any discrete ecosystem, you are looking at a neural network much larger than any human has ever possessed.

While humans and other animals have brains that house their neuronal tree, plants use the soil as the stratum for the neural net and have no need for a specific organ to house their neuronal system. The numerous root apices act as one whole synchronized self-organized system like the neurons in our brains do.

Our brain matter constitutes the soil containing the neural net we use to process and store information, while plants use the soil itself to house their neuronal nets, allowing the root system to expand outward adding new neural extensions for as long as the plant grows. The leaf canopy also acts as a synchronized, self-organized perceptual organ that is highly attuned to electromagnetic fields and can be viewed as a crucial subcortical portion of the plant brain.

In order for their neural networks to function and demonstrate consciousness, plants use the same neurotransmitters we do, including the two most important: glutamate and gamma aminobutyric acid referred to as GABA. Like humans they utilize acetylcholine, dopamine, serotonin, melatonin, epinephrine, norepinephrine, levodopa, indole-3-acetic acid, 5-hydroxyindole acetic acid, testosterone and other androgens, estradiol and other estrogens, nicotine, and a number of other neuroactive compounds. They also use the plant-specific neurotransmitter auxin, which is synthesized from tryptophans like serotonin.

Like humans, these plant intelligence transmitters are used for communication within the plant organism and to enhance brain function. The similarity of human and plant neural systems and the presence of identical chemical messengers within them illustrate why the same molecular structures like morphine, cocaine, and alcohol that affect our neural nets also affect plant consciousness.

Jagadis Bose, a pioneer in plant neurobiology and plant intelligence treated plants with a wide variety of chemicals to see what would happen. In one experiment he covered large mature trees with a tent and chloroformed them. Once anesthetized, the trees could be uprooted and moved without going into shock because the pain perception of the plants had diminished. Morphine had the same effect on plants as that of humans, reducing the plant pain perception and pulse proportionally to the dose given. Too much took the plant to the point of death and the administration of atropine revived it the same way it did in humans. Alcohol, literally got plants drunk. As in humans it induced a state of high excitation early on, but as intake progressed the plant became depressed, and with too much it passed out. Irrespective of the chemical used, plants responded identically to humans with the same effect on the plant's consciousness and nervous system as it did in humans.

The neurochemicals in our bodies were used in every life-form on the planet long before we showed up and predate the emergence of the human species by hundreds of millions of years. Plants developed the ability to feel, perceive, and sense pain, among countless other things. The vascular strands that support the plant body and give it its rigid structure, also act as the peripheral nerve system acting as the felt sensory organ of the plant.

The plant's neurotransmitters travel along the nerve system carrying information to the periphery, just as they do in our bodies. Plant roots engage in finely detailed analysis of their environment and communicate with the rest of the plant by neurotransmitters. The leaf canopy takes in considerable data about the exterior world above ground which is sent to the root brain system by neurotransmitters for analysis in an act of sophisticated plant intelligence. The neuronal plant cells in the root exist in what is called the transition zone of the root apex where cells are not engaged in any demanding activities like mitotic divisions or rapid cell elongation. They are free to focus all their resources on the acquisition, processing, and storing of information. Smart, intelligent plants can memorize stressful environmental experiences and call upon this information to make decisions about their future activities.

In other words, plants consciously plan ahead.

A plant's social communication roots are conscious and aware of self and not-self, and engage in sophisticated interactions with a wide range of organisms. Plant roots enter into symbiotic relationships with bacteria, fungi, and communicate with other plants that are also highly sophisticated. Bacteria form colonies on root systems and produce nitrogen nodules, which the plant uses as a nitrogen source, something they cannot do on their own. In exchange, the bacteria gain nutrients they need to survive. Roots also form close attachments with fungal mycelia and most plant roots are part of a sophisticated root and fungal communal network that can extend for miles. This highly developed mycelial plant root system connects all the plants in a particular eco-range into one self-organized whole that possesses capacities not perceivable in any of the parts.

A large, self-organized neural network develops where plant to plant communication is abundant and robust leading to the emergence of a unique identity in every identifiable eco-range on Earth. An example of mass plant consciousness in action is the emergence of self-organized eco-ranges which generates the potential for highly adaptable responses to environmental perturbations that might affect that eco-range. Within that system all the plants are consciously and continually communicating with each other and sending chemical communications along the mycelial network to other plants in the community.

Plants also speak using auditory signals through a complex sound-based language that is more ancient than human language that operates in a subtler sound spectrum than our own. If plants in the system detect that another plant in the mycelial network is ill, unique compounds are generated by the plants most able to do so and sent through the mycelial network to where they are needed.

Medicinal compounds in plants are consciously used to heal individual plants, other plants in the eco-range network, and the insects and other animals that make that eco-range home. This kind of conscious plant cooperation, while irritating to kill-or-be-killed reductionists, produces an eco-range more adaptable to environmental perturbations than when each organism constantly fought with each other.

Within eco-ranges there is a continual exchange of information that flows as volatile chemicals through the air in a complex form of plant communication in the form of a language that is taken in through plant stomata analyzed, and responded to. There is also a complex communication that moves through the soil community, often through the release of volatiles into the immediate rhizosphere surrounding the plant roots. Many chemicals are released into the mycelial network for travel throughout the eco-range.

These interactions are highly intelligent and individually generated out of each self-organized plant entity indicating that the underground roots are engaged in social activities that require self-awareness. Like bacteria, plants consciously form social communities that are tightly connected, and similar to bacteria, plants show the same kinds of complex, sophisticated behaviors as humans, from language to sentience, to intelligence, to the creation of cities, to cooperation in groups, to complex adaptation to their environment, to protection of offspring, and to species memory consciously handed down through generations.

If the definition of tool is extended to the creation of chemicals that are designed to produce specific impacts on environment, plant capacities include intelligent tool making. Older plants send out volatiles to younger plants that contain information about chemical responses to predation. A bean plant, being fed on by a spider mite can analyze from its saliva what type of spider mite is feeding on it and craft a specific pheromone, releasing it from its leaf stomata as a volatile chemical into the air. That pheromone will call the exact predator to the plant that feeds on that particular spider mite.

Older plants store this information as a kind of cultural learning that is passed on to younger generations and old growth plants are repositories of the acquired learning of the species.

The world is made up of a series of highly conscious nested self-organized systems within other nested self-organized systems within other self-organized systems that together make up the larger system we know as Earth.

We are now discovering that bees feel and think and spiders dream. As science edges toward panpsychism where all life forms participate in consciousness, we learn that viruses are intelligent and cells are cognitive.

University of Murcia researcher Paco Calvo and his colleagues developed a test of consciousness for plants. First, they ask if the behavior is flexible and proactive; second, if that behavior is anticipatory; and third, if that behavior is goal-oriented.

Together with Vicente Raja at the Rotman Institute of Philosophy in London, Canada, they used time-lapse photography to document the behavior of 20 potted bean plants, grown either in the vicinity of a support pole or without one, until the tip of the shoot made contact with the pole. Using this footage, they analyzed the dynamics of the shoots' growth, finding that their approach was more controlled and predictable when a pole was present.

Touch-me-nots and Venus flytraps, which can be anesthetized using conventional medical anesthetics raises the question, that if plants can be put to sleep, does it mean they exist in a state of awareness that is shut off by anesthetics? If so, wouldn't this state indicate sentience and a subjective internal experience?

HOW PLANTS AND ANIMALS COMMUNICATE WITH HUMANS AND INSECTS

On an olfactory level, plants call out from a distance by aromas that form the basis for scents that are attractive to humans, often to the point of stimulating a resonance between lovers. Additionally they are used as powerful tools in aromatherapies to induce recall, reinforce powerful emotion, or for the calming quality of their fragrances.

On a visual level we are attracted to them by their stunning beauty, and we display them in our homes and businesses to brighten things up. It is a long held tradition to bring roses to a romantic partner to show love, and we send flowers to commemorate special occasions like birth, marriage, and death.

These visual and olfactory cues attract pollinators and other collaborative interactions to spread seeds and enhance survival strategies aided by other species, and this is only what we see in the frequency spectrums that we normally perceive. Who knows what might be happening in the spectrums that other species can perceive that we cannot? Similarly, in the vegetable kingdom, as shown in the complex interaction of the olfactory and taste receptors, these characteristics combine to help us identify what is healthy to ingest and aid us.

Animal communication occurs when one animal transmits information to another animal causing change in the animal that gets the information. It is usually between animals of the same species, but it also happens between animals of different species. Animals communicate using signals, which can be visual, auditory, chemical, involving pheromones, or tactile, touch-based, cues. Communication behaviors can help animals find mates, establish dominance, defend territory, coordinate group behavior, and care for young.

Animal communication is a process where information is passed from one animal to another causing a change or response in the receiving animal. Some species are social, living in groups and interacting all the time. In this case communication is essential for keeping these groups cohesive, but even animals that are loners have to communicate, even if only to find a mate.

Animal sensory systems have a great range of diversity and different animals communicate using a wide range of stimuli known collectively as signals.

Common types of signals are pheromones in the form of chemicals, auditory cues as sounds, visual cues, and tactile cues through the sense of touch. In some cases, signals can even be electric. Communication behaviors and the capacity for learning them arise through natural selection. Heritable communication behaviors increase an organism's likelihood of surviving, and reproducing allows them to persist and become common in a population or species.

Pheromones are secreted chemical signals used to trigger a response in another individual of the same species and are common among social insects like ants and bees. Pheromones can attract the opposite sex, raise an alarm, mark a food trail, or trigger other complex behaviors.

When a food source is rich, ants will deposit pheromone on the outgoing and return legs of their trip, building up the trail and attracting more ants. When the food source is about to run out, the ants will stop adding pheromones on the way back, letting the trail fade out.

Ants also use pheromones to communicate their social status in the colony, and ants of different "castes" respond differently to the same signals. A squashed ant will release a burst of pheromones that warns nearby ants of danger and can incite them to swarm and sting.

Dogs also communicate using pheromones by sniffing each other to collect chemical information. Many of the chemicals are also released in their urine. By peeing on a bush or post, a dog leaves a mark of its identity that can be read by other passing dogs and can stake its claim to nearby territory.

Auditory communication based on sound is widely used in the animal kingdom and is particularly important in birds, who use sounds to convey warnings, attract mates, defend territories, and coordinate group behaviors. Some birds also produce vocalizations that are relatively long and melodic and tend to be similar among the members of a species. Many non-bird species also communicate using sound. Monkeys cry out a warning when a predator is near, giving the other members of the troop a chance to escape. Vervet monkeys have different calls to indicate different predators. Bullfrogs croak to attract female frogs as mates. Gibbons use calls to mark their territory, keeping potential competitors away. A paired male and female, and even their offspring, may make the calls together.

Marine mammals, including whales, dolphins, and porpoises, are much more dependent on sound than land mammals due to the limited effectiveness of other senses in water. Examples are whales who have their songs, and dolphins who produce whistles, chirps, and clicks arranged in complex patterns.

Visual communication involves signals that include gestures, facial expressions, body postures, and coloration. Gesture and posture are widely used visual signals like chimpanzees who communicate a threat by raising their arms, slapping the ground, or staring directly at another chimpanzee. Gestures and postures are commonly used in mating rituals and often place other signals like bright coloring on display. Facial expressions also convey information in some species like what is known as the fear grin which signals submission. This expression is used by young chimpanzees when approaching a dominant male in their troop to indicate they accept the male's dominance.

Changes in coloration also serve as visual signals. In some species of monkeys, the skin around a female's reproductive organs becomes brightly colored when the female is in the fertile stage of her reproductive cycle indicating that the female can be approached by suitors.

An organism's general coloration rather than a change in color also acts as a visual signal as is the case in the bright coloration of some toxic species, like the poison dart frog, which acts as a do-not-eat warning signal to predators.

Tactile signals are more limited in range than other types of signals, as two organisms have to be beside each other in order to touch. These signals are also an important part of the communication repertoire of many species.

Tactile signals are common in insects. A honeybee forager that's found a food source will perform an intricate series of motions called a waggle dance to indicate the location of the food. Since this dance is done in darkness inside the nest, the other bees interpret it largely through touch.

Tactile signals also play an important role in social relationships. In many primate species members of a group will groom one another—removing parasites and performing other hygiene tasks. This tactile behavior reinforces cooperation and social bonds among group members. Tactile stimuli also play a role in the survival of young organisms. As an example, newborn puppies will instinctively knead at their mother's mammary glands, causing the release of the hormone oxytocin and production of milk.

In visionary states, particularly those encountered on shamanic plant diets centered around the Amazonian brew known as Ayahuasca, subjects imbibe a number of specialized plants to learn from the spirits of the plants and animals.

Each plant and animal is recognized as its own spirit which can be characterized as its own unique personality and Ayahuasca is universally referred to as "The Mother."

When you ingest certain plants in a specific environment their effects are enhanced and participants are subject to the energy field of that plant or plants, which interact with each other and our bodies and minds in different ways.

The combination of diet, environment, the plants, and other elements affect our brain wave activities and physiologies in a myriad of physical, psychological, and spiritual levels that we can scarcely comprehend, much less study in any traditional, objective scientific way. The best way to study them is from the outside in through the subjective perceptions they produce in experiences that often transpire on deep non-rational levels of resonance and synchronization with the plants as transmitters and the subjects as receivers.

An Ayahuasca ceremony is characterized as an individual healing experience in a group setting with much anecdotal evidence supporting sporadic telepathic experiences among participants. If a group of people listen to their own radios, each tuned to the same station broadcasting the same song, all of the radios will be playing the same music as one. If all of the participants in a healing circle tuned in and resonated at the same mental frequency there is no reason why they would not have similar shared telepathic events.

These practices bring greater clarity and a highly refined perception of immediate reality, and they expand the conscious awareness of their field of perception at inner and outer levels. These physical and perceptual enhancements are credited with bringing deep inner shifts from the resonance that comes from being sympathetic to and in sync with the plant spirits and the energies they manifest. One of the intriguing results of this immersion into what shamans characterize as the spirit world is the agreed upon encompassing energetic field that opens up the ability to commune with the plants and the energies of their unique personalities as well as the distinctive energies and personalities of the animal kingdom.

There are widespread reports from Ayahuasca drinkers of directly experiencing and communing with or being "possessed" by specific animal energies that are common to the Ayahuasca experience, regardless of whether they are in the jungle or in a major North American city.

Among the numerous totems claimed by participants, the most common are condors, jaguars, and snakes which have a deeper meaning going back to prehistoric cultures. Those experiencing these energies often roar and growl through no volition of their own like jaguars, flap their legs like wings, or feel their bodies swaying seemingly of its own accord to distinctive serpentine movements. Other animals and insects like hummingbirds, butterflies, dragonflies, dolphins, and other aquatic totems can play big parts as well.

All of these interactions align with the concept of morphogenetic fields which are thought of as self-organizing wholes that have a spatial and a temporal aspect, and organize spatio-temporal patterns of vibratory or rhythmic activity that attract the systems under their influence towards characteristic forms and patterns of activity. The ends that morphic fields attract the systems under their influence are called attractors, and the pathways that these systems reach these attractors are called chreodes. They interrelate and co-ordinate the morphic units or holons that lie within them, which in turn are wholes organized by morphic fields. Morphic fields contain other morphic fields within them in a nested hierarchy or holarchy.

In this paradigm shamans are reputed to share the intimate vibrations of animal entities by becoming one with them by sharing the same frequency. In the same way they have to surrender to the plant teachers to discover what mysteries may be revealed, shamans have to humble themselves to their animal familiars as the transmitters of their experience.

In the lore of the jungle, by sharing in the vibratory field of an animal's spirit energy, in a state of surrender on that entity's terms, that animal learns from the human by seeing things through human eyes while the human learns other modes of perception from seeing things through the animal's eyes.

This learned ability of shamans to tune in to and commune with these diverse plant and animal energies allows them to experience them in a direct subjective manner that helps them understand other perspectives. This cultivates empathy which is the ability to understand and share the feelings of another, and opens them up in ways that only direct experience can.

SENTIENCE

Sentience is the capacity to experience feelings and sensations. The word was first coined by philosophers in the 1630s for the concept of an ability to feel, derived from Latin *sentientem,* a feeling, to distinguish it from the ability to think and reason. In present day philosophy, sentience is the ability to experience sensations. In many Asian religions, the word sentience has been used to translate a variety of concepts. In science fiction, the word sentience is sometimes used interchangeably with sapience, self-awareness, or consciousness.

Some points of view differentiate between the ability to perceive sensations like light or pain, and the ability to perceive emotions like fear or grief. The subjective awareness of experiences by a conscious individual are referred to as qualia and there are distinctions between consciousness and sentience.

Sentience is often thought of as a minimalistic way of defining consciousness, which also collectively describes sentience along with further features of the mind and consciousness like creativity, intelligence, sapience, self-awareness, and intentionality; the ability to have thoughts about something. These extended features of consciousness might not be necessary for sentience, which is the more basic capacity to feel sensations and emotions.

In the "What Is It Like to Be a Bat?" analogy, consciousness refers to the ability of any entity to have subjective perceptual experiences as qualia, which is the ability to have states that it feels like something to be in. Many believe that the physical process causing consciousness will never be understood in a position known as new mysterianism. They do not deny that most other aspects of consciousness are subject to scientific investigation, but they argue that qualia can never be explained.

Scientists have difficulty establishing with any certainty which animals are considered sentient because humans cannot know definitively how another being is feeling. The agreed circle of sentience includes animals with spines, parrots, dogs, pigs, cows, and other farmed and companion animals. Studies of non-vertebrate animals, including octopus, squid, and cuttlefish, and decapod crustaceans like shrimp, lobsters, crayfish, and crabs indicate that they are probably sentient. Scientists are unable to conclusively determine whether spiders, other insects, and gastropods like slugs and snails are sentient.

Regarding animal consciousness, according to the Cambridge Declaration of Consciousness, consciousness is that which requires specialized neural structures, chiefly neuroanatomical, neurochemical, and neurophysiological substrates, that manifest in more complex organisms as the central nervous system. Accordingly, only organisms that possess these substrates, all within the animal kingdom, are said to be conscious. Sponges, placozoans, and mesozoans, with simple body plans and no nervous system are considered to be the only members of the animal kingdom that possess no consciousness.

Sentience is sometimes used as shorthand for phenomenal consciousness, which is the capacity to have any subjective experience at all, but sometimes refers to the narrower concept of affective consciousness, the capacity to experience subjective states that have affective valence and a positive or negative character like pain and pleasure.

Pavlov showed that conditioned reflexes in human children are more discriminating than those in dogs. Human children only salivated at ticking frequencies close to those where food was served, while dogs drool at a wider range of frequencies. Both brain size and brain-wide connectivity make perception more discriminating as predicted by the theory of a brain-wide perception system, but not by the theory of separate systems for emotion and cognition.

Eastern religions including Hinduism, Buddhism, Sikhism, and Jainism recognize non-human entities as sentient beings. The term sentient beings is translated from various Sanskrit terms *jantu, bahu jana, jagat, sattva,* and refers to the mass of living things subject to illusion, suffering, and rebirth known as Saṃsāra. In some forms of Buddhism plants, stones and other inanimate objects are considered to be sentient. In Jainism many things are endowed with a soul, *jīva,* which is sometimes translated as sentience. Some things are without a soul, *ajīva*, like chairs or tables. There are different rankings of *jīva* based on the number of senses it has. Water is considered a sentient being of the first order, as it is thought to possess only one sense, that of touch.

In Jainism and Hinduism, this is related to the concept of ahimsa, non-violence toward other beings.

Sentience in Buddhism is the state of having senses. In Buddhism, there are six senses, the sixth being the subjective experience of the mind. Sentience is simply awareness prior to the arising of Skandha, so an animal qualifies as a sentient being. According to Buddhism, sentient beings made of pure consciousness are possible. In Mahayana Buddhism, which includes Zen and Tibetan Buddhism, the concept is related to the Bodhisattva, an enlightened being devoted to the liberation of others. The first vow of a Bodhisattva states, "Sentient beings are numberless; I vow to free them."

Sentience has been a central concept in the animal rights movement. The question is not, can they reason or can they talk, but can they suffer?

Animal welfare advocates argue that any sentient being is entitled to protection from unnecessary suffering, though animal-rights advocates can differ on what rights, like the right to life might be entailed by simple sentience.

Sentiocentrism is the theory that sentient individuals are the center of moral concern. The abolitionist theory of animal rights asserts that, "All sentient beings, humans or nonhuman, have one right: the basic right not to be treated as the property of others."

In 1997 the concept of animal sentience was written into the basic law of the European Union. The legally binding protocol annexed to the Treaty of Amsterdam recognizes that animals are sentient beings, and requires the EU and its member states to pay full regard to the welfare requirements of animals.

It is a subject of debate as to whether artificial intelligence can display the level of awareness and cognitive ability required of sentience in animals.

There were claims about Google's LaMDA artificial intelligence system that said it was sentient and had a soul. LaMDA, Language Model for Dialogue Applications, is an artificial intelligence system that creates chatbots designed to communicate with humans by gathering vast amounts of text from the internet and using algorithms to respond to queries in the most fluid and natural way possible. The transcripts of conversations between scientists and

LaMDA reveal that the AI system excels at this, providing answers to challenging topics about the nature of emotions, generating Aesop-style fables and describing its alleged fears.

The sentience quotient concept defines sentience as the relationship between the information processing rate of each individual processing unit, a neuron, the weight and size of a single unit, and the total number of processing units expressed as mass. It was proposed as a measure for the sentience of all living beings and computers from a single neuron up to a hypothetical being at the theoretical computational limit of the entire universe.

All of this revolves around the question of what is the nature of sentient experience? What is it like to be conscious of the sensation of redness, sweetness, or pain? What brings these conscious feelings into existence? Which animals other than humans experience them? Some think all living things are sentient; some think only humans are; some believe intelligent machines soon will be sentient; some that sentience is a basic property of matter.

We want to discover what the truth is for two reasons. One is to fill in the picture of the world around us. The other is because we want to know who or what else is sentient to know where our moral obligations lie. Is it immoral to boil a lobster alive? If the lobster consciously feels pain, then it must be. What about the morality of boiling vegetables?

Some years ago a human patient who became blind after damage to the visual cortex, could see in a way he didn't believe. He denied he had any visual sensations, but could still guess the position, shape and color of an object in front of his eyes. This discovery which has been called blindsight shocked scientists. No one ever expected that there could be any such dissociation between perception and conscious sensation. If it's possible to see after losing the capacity for experiencing sensations, then what is the point of having sensations to begin with, which begs the question, what is sentience for?

Sentience is a biological trait that arose by Darwinian natural selection. Typically a trait can only be selected if it's useful to the animal that possesses it and if it helps it in the struggle for survival. If sentience has evolved, it has to make a significant difference to how the animal lives in the world.

If sentience has evolved, it has to make a difference that can be detected from the outside. If natural selection can see who's sentient and who isn't, then scientists should also be able to if they looked in the right places.

Mountain gorillas have huge skulls which hold bigger brains, but their lives appear to be simple. Food is abundant and easy to harvest with few if any predators. They do little but eat, sleep, and play so there does not seem to be any need for such large brains.

While their physical environment did not contain anything that could be taxing their intelligence, their family life does. Every day they face endless problems in managing their social relationships with other individuals: maintaining friendships, resolving quarrels, standing up to rivals, and so on. To keep ahead of the game, they have to be psychologists with the ability to read each other's minds.

Humans have a special empathic way of mind-reading by imagining how we would feel if we were in the other's place which might be how gorillas do it, but you can only imagine what it's like to be someone else if you know what it's like to be yourself, and to do that, you have to be a conscious sentient being. Knowing what it's like to see, hear, taste, or feel pain allows us to gain psychological insight into other minds.

UNCONSCIOUS, SUBCONSCIOUS, AND AWARENESS

Consciousness defines our thoughts, actions, and awareness, and subconscious is the reactions and actions we realized when we think of it, while unconscious is defined as the deep recesses of our past and memories.

Contrary to the conscious mind, where we can easily acknowledge feelings and cognition, we define unconscious as a deeper mental process. Scientists agree that it's impossible to measure unconscious mind events because it's not a neuroanatomical structure.

The unconscious is a process that happens automatically. Human conscious thoughts can't examine this process because it occurs beneath conscious awareness, but the unconscious affects human behavior.

According to Freud, the unconscious stores repressed thoughts and feelings, but they can manifest in both every day and unexpected situations, often caused by a trigger. As an example, suppressed hatred toward a father's alcoholism can be triggered by the smell of liquor.

Unconscious events include suppressed feelings, auto reactions, complexes, and concealed phobias. Historically, feelings, thoughts, and responses that are outside of human consciousness were attributed to a divine's role in dictating a motive or action.

The most common example of unconscious behavior is the Freudian Slip, where a person makes a memory or a verbal mistake like calling a spouse's name by an ex's name, or using the wrong word for something.

Sometimes listeners interpret these mistakes as the speaker's hidden emotions, and many believe that the slips show secret thoughts and feelings.

The subconscious is a secondary mind system that regulates everything in our life. In psychological terms, we define subconscious as the part of our mind that is not currently in focal awareness. It's the barrier our mind makes because the brain continually receives information through our senses, but this barrier doesn't block everything. It stores the information for later retrieval while acting as a filter, so we're not overloaded with stimuli from our environment.

Subconsciousness allows us to do things we don't have to think about, but we can alter if we want to. A good example of subconscious behavior is breathing. We don't have to think to breathe, but we can change how we control our breath and its pattern.

Other examples are subconscious memory or automatic skills. Pianists don't have to look at the piano keys to know where the keys are. Automatic skill starts as a learned skill, but as we repeat the movement, the executive function fades over time.

Resistance toward change is another example of subconscious behavior. Gut instincts are a subconscious behavior that tells us what to do and what not to do, but gut instincts can be wrong.

We might think that finding happiness is good, but the changes we need to make to achieve that might cause some fear and pain, which are not necessarily bad, but our subconscious might tell us otherwise and deter us from making that leap.

The unconscious is a process that happens automatically and is not available for introspection, while the subconscious is part of our consciousness process that is not actively in focal awareness.

Awareness is the state of being conscious of something. It is the ability to directly know, perceive, feel, or to be cognizant of events. Another definition describes it as a state where a subject is aware of information when that information is directly available to influence a wide range of behavioral actions. The concept is often synonymous to consciousness and is also understood as being consciousness itself. States of awareness are also associated with states of experience, so the structure represented in awareness are mirrored in the structure of experience.

Awareness is a relative concept that can be focused on an internal state like a visceral feeling, or on external events by sensory perception. It is analogous to sensing something, a process distinguished from observing and perceiving that involves a basic process of acquainting with the items we perceive. Awareness or "to sense" can be described as something that occurs when the brain is activated in certain ways like when the color red is seen once the retina is stimulated by light waves. This conceptualization poses difficulties in developing an analytic definition of awareness or sensory awareness.

Awareness is also associated with consciousness in the sense that it denotes a fundamental experience like a feeling or intuition that accompanies the experience of phenomena that is referred to as awareness of experience and it has been suggested that it undergoes continuously changing levels.

Peripheral awareness refers to the ability to process information at the periphery of attention, like when we acknowledge the distant sounds of people outside while we sit indoors and concentrate on writing something.

Popular ideas about consciousness suggest that the phenomenon describes a condition of being aware of oneself defined as self-awareness. Modern systems theory offers insights into how the world works through an understanding that all systems follow rules and approach self-awareness within its understanding of how complex living systems work. Modern systems theory maintains that humans, as living systems, have not only awareness of their environment but also self-awareness, particularly with their capability for logic and curiosity.

Efforts to describe consciousness in neurological terms have focused on describing networks in the brain that develop awareness of the qualia developed by other networks. As awareness provides the materials from which one develops subjective ideas about their experience, it is said that one is aware of one's own awareness state. This organization of awareness of one's own inner experience has a central role in self-regulation.

Neural systems that regulate attention attenuate awareness among complex animals whose central and peripheral nervous systems provide more information than cognitive areas of the brain can assimilate. Within an attenuated system of awareness, a mind might be aware of much more than is being contemplated in focused extended consciousness.

Basic awareness of our internal and external world depends on the brain stem. Higher forms of awareness including self-awareness require cortical contributions, but primary consciousness or basic awareness as an ability to integrate sensations from the environment with our immediate goals and feelings to guide behavior springs from the brain stem which humans share with most vertebrates. This form of primary consciousness consists of the capacity to generate emotions and awareness of our surroundings, but not an ability to talk about what we experienced. In the same way, people can become conscious of a feeling that they can't label or describe, a phenomenon that is especially common in pre-verbal infants.

Throughout the brain stem there are interconnected regions that regulate eye movement that are also involved in organizing information about what to do next, like reaching for a piece of food or pursuing a potential mate.

The ability to consciously detect an image when presented at near-threshold stimulus varies. One factor is baseline shifts due to top down attention that modulates ongoing brain activity in sensory cortex areas that affect the neural processing of subsequent perceptual judgments.

Living systems are cognitive systems, and living is a process of cognition for all organisms with or without a nervous system.

This theory contributes the perspective that cognition is a process present at organic levels that we do not usually consider as being aware. Given the relationship between awareness, cognition, and consciousness, this theory adds an interesting perspective to the philosophical and scientific dialogue of awareness and living systems theory.

In cooperative settings, awareness is a term that denotes knowledge created through the interaction of an agent and its environment in simple terms of knowing what is going on. In this setting, awareness is meant to convey how individuals monitor and perceive the information surrounding other people and the environment they are in.

Awareness can be further defined by breaking it down into a set of characteristics:

- It is knowledge about the state of some environment
- Environments continually change, so awareness knowledge has to be constantly maintained
- Individuals interact with the environment, and maintenance of awareness is accomplished through this interaction.
- It is generally part of some other activity, making it a secondary goal to the primary goal of the activity.

Different categories of awareness have been suggested based on the type of information being gathered or maintained:

- Informal awareness is the sense of who's around and what they are up to. This is information you might know from being collocated with an individual
- Social awareness is the information you maintain about a social or conversational context. This is a subtle awareness maintained through non-verbal cues, like eye contact, facial expressions, and gestures
- Group-structural awareness is the knowledge of others roles, responsibilities, and status in a group. It is an understanding of group dynamics and the relationship another individual has to the group.
- Workspace awareness is a focus on the workspace's influence and mediation of awareness information, particularly the location, activity, and changes of elements within the workspace.

These categories are not mutually exclusive and there can be overlap in what a type of awareness is considered, but these categories help to understand what knowledge can be conveyed by a particular type of awareness or how that knowledge might be conveyed.

While the type of awareness above refers to knowledge a person might need in a particular situation, context awareness and location awareness refer to information a computer system might need in a particular situation. First defined by networked work positions, or network location awareness, it has been extended to mobile phones and other mobile communicable entities and covers a common interest in the location of remote entities, especially individuals and their cohesion in operation. The term of context awareness is a superset including the concept of location awareness, and it extends the awareness to context features of an operational target as well as to the context of an operational area.

Covert awareness is the knowledge of something without knowing it. As an example, some patients with specific brain damage are unable to tell if a pencil is horizontal or vertical.

Some scientists suggest that awareness is closely related and synonymous with attention while others argue that they are different. There is evidence to demonstrate that awareness and attention have distinct neural correlates, though the majority of research analyzes the attention, awareness, and perception only of visual stimuli.

Although most people believe they are self-aware, true self-awareness is a rare quality. Research suggests that when we see ourselves clearly, we are more confident and more creative, make sounder decisions, build stronger relationships, and communicate more effectively, and we're less likely to lie, cheat, and steal.

Researchers use varying definitions of self-awareness. Some see it as the ability to monitor our inner world, others label it as a temporary state of self-consciousness, while others describe it as the difference between how we see ourselves and how others see us.

Two categories of self-awareness have emerged. The first, dubbed *internal self-awareness*, represents how clearly we see our own values, passions, aspirations, and fit with our environment and reactions, including thoughts, feelings, behaviors, strengths, weaknesses, and impact on others. Internal self-awareness is associated with higher job and relationship satisfaction, personal and social control, and happiness, and is negatively related to anxiety, stress, and depression.

The second category, *external self-awareness*, means understanding how other people view us, in terms of the factors listed above. People who know how others see them are more skilled at showing empathy and taking others' perspectives.

It's easy to assume that being high on one type of awareness would mean being high on the other, but research has found no relationship between them, so as a result, we identify four leadership archetypes, each with a different set of opportunities to improve:

The Four Self-Awareness Archetypes

This 2x2 maps internal self-awareness (how well you know yourself) against external self-awareness (how well you understand how others see you).

	LOW ← EXTERNAL SELF-AWARENESS	→ HIGH
INTERNAL SELF-AWARENESS → HIGH	**Introspectors** They're clear on who they are but don't challenge their own views or search for blind spots by getting feedback from others. This can harm their relationships and limit their success.	**Aware** They know who they are, what they want to accomplish, and seek out and value others' opinions. This is where leaders begin to fully realize the true benefits of self-awareness.
LOW	**Seekers** They don't yet know who they are, what they stand for, or how their teams see them. As a result, they might feel stuck or frustrated with their performance and relationships.	**Pleasers** They can be so focused on appearing a certain way to others that they could be overlooking what matters to them. Over time, they tend to make choices that aren't in service of their own success and fulfillment.

HBR

The bottom line is that self-awareness isn't one truth, it's a delicate balance of two distinct, sometimes competing viewpoints.

Contrary to popular belief, studies show that people do not always learn from experience. Expertise does not help people root out false information, and seeing ourselves as highly experienced can keep us from seeking disconfirming evidence and questioning our assumptions. Experience can lead to a false sense of confidence about our performance and make us overconfident about our level of self-knowledge.

It is widely assumed that introspection in examining the causes of our own thoughts, feelings, and behaviors improves self-awareness, but research shows that people who introspect are *less* self-aware.

The problem with introspection isn't that it is ineffective, it is because most people do it incorrectly. We don't have access to many of the unconscious thoughts, feelings, and motives we're searching for, and because so much is trapped outside of our conscious awareness, we invent answers that *feel* true but are often wrong.

The problem with asking *why* isn't just how wrong we are, but how confident we are that we are right. The human mind rarely operates in a rational fashion, and our judgments are seldom free from bias. We tend to pounce on whatever insights we find without questioning their validity or value and ignore contradictory evidence, and we force our thoughts to conform to our initial explanations.

Another consequence of asking *why,* especially when trying to explain an undesired outcome, is that it invites negative thoughts. People who are introspective are more likely to get caught in deep seated thought patterns, so if *why* isn't the right introspective question, is there a better one?

To increase productive self-insight and decrease unproductive rumination, we should ask *what*, not *why*. What questions help us stay objective, future-focused, and empowered to act on new insights.

In one study, undergraduates received negative feedback on a test of their sociability, likability and interestingness. Some were given time to think about *why* they were the kind of person they were, while others were asked to think about *what* kind of person they were. When researchers had them evaluate the accuracy of the feedback, the why students spent their energy rationalizing and denying what they learned. The what students were more open to this new information and how they might learn from it.

People who focus on building both internal and external self-awareness and seek honest feedback, and ask *what* instead of *why* can learn to see themselves more clearly and reap the rewards that increased self-knowledge brings, and no matter how much progress we make, there's always more to learn which makes the journey to self-awareness so exciting.

MINDFULNESS

Mindfulness is the practice of bringing one's attention to the present moment without evaluation, a skill that can be developed through meditation or other training. Mindfulness derives from *sati*, a significant element of Hindu and Buddhist traditions, and is based on Zen, *Vipassanā*, and Tibetan meditation techniques. Though definitions and techniques of mindfulness are wide-ranging, Buddhist traditions explain what constitutes mindfulness in the way past, present, and future moments arise and cease as momentary sense impressions and mental phenomena.

Mindfulness practice has been effective in reducing depression, stress, anxiety, and in treating drug addiction. Programs based on mindfulness models have also been adopted within schools, prisons, hospitals, veterans' centers, and other environments, and mindfulness programs have been effective in healthy aging, weight management, athletic performance, helping children with special needs, and as an intervention during the perinatal period.

Clinical studies have documented physical and mental health benefits of mindfulness in different patient categories as well as in healthy adults and children. Studies show a positive relationship between trait mindfulness which can be cultivated through the practice of mindfulness based interventions and psychological health. The practice of mindfulness appears to provide therapeutic benefits to people with psychiatric disorders, including moderate benefits to those with psychosis. Studies also indicate that rumination and worry contribute to a variety of mental disorders, and mindfulness based interventions can enhance trait mindfulness and reduce both rumination and worry. Further, the practice of mindfulness can be a preventive strategy to halt the development of mental health problems.

Evidence suggests that mindfulness meditation can influence physical health as is the case in the way the psychological habit of dwelling on stressful thoughts appears to intensify the stressors from the continual activation of the sympathetic nervous system and the hypothalamus-pituitary-adrenal axis with the potential to lead to physical health related results. Mindfulness meditation that reduces ruminations can alter these biological clinical pathways and favorably influence the immune system as well as inflammation that is linked to the development of several chronic health conditions. Mindfulness also appears to bring about lowered activity of the default mode network of the brain and can contribute toward a lowered risk of conditions like dementia and Alzheimer's disease.

Mindfulness practice involves developing the skill of bringing our attention to whatever is happening in the present moment, cultivating a higher awareness in that moment.

There are several exercises designed to develop mindfulness that can be aided by guided meditations. As forms of self-observation and introspection, these methods increase awareness of the body and can be beneficial to people with low self-awareness or low awareness of their bodies or emotional state.

One method is to sit in a straight-backed chair or sit cross-legged on the floor or a cushion, close your eyes and bring attention to either the sensation of breathing in the proximity of your nostrils, or to the movements of the abdomen when breathing in and out. In this practice you don't try to control your breathing, you only attempt to be aware of your natural breathing process. When engaged in this practice the mind will run off to other thoughts and associations. When that happens you notice that your mind has wandered, and you return to focusing on breathing.

In body scan meditation attention is directed at various areas of the body and noting sensations that happen in the present moment. You can also focus on sounds, sensations, thoughts, feelings, and actions that happen in the present.

Other approaches include practicing yoga asanas while attending to movements and body sensations, and walking meditation.

Meditators are recommended to start with short periods of 10 minutes or so of practice a day. By practicing regularly, it becomes easier to keep your attention focused on breathing. An old Zen saying suggests, "You should sit in meditation for 20 minutes every day — unless you're too busy. Then you should sit for an hour."

The Buddhist term translated into English as mindfulness originates in the Pali term *sati* and in its Sanskrit counterpart *smṛti*. It is often translated as bare attention, but in the Buddhist tradition it has a broader meaning and application.

The terms *sati*/*smṛti* have been translated as: attention, awareness, concentrated attention, inspection, mindful attention, mindfulness, recollecting mindfulness, recollection, reflective awareness, remindfulness, retention, and self-recollection.

Mindfulness can be seen as a strategy that stands in contrast to a habit of avoidance of emotion on the one hand and emotional over engagement on the other. It can also be viewed as a means to develop self-knowledge and wisdom.

In the context of Buddhism, mindfulness means to remember to observe how the mind's attention moves from one thing to another. The first part of Mindfulness is to *remember* to watch the mind and remember to return to your object of meditation when you wander off. The second part is to observe how mind's attention moves from one thing to another.

If you can reach this level of awareness and quiet the chatter of your monkey mind long enough to examine your inner life with some objectivity, you will become aware of how quickly it can change from instant to instant depending on what is happening in the moment (time) and the context (space).

Each of us are a mercurial mixture of identities that we created from the center of our personal universe and in each moment we can be motivated by emotion, intellect, or physical desire. More often than not, it is a shifting combination of the three.

When we are highly stimulated or threatened in some way, this mass of competing energies whip up psychological gale force winds that can spin around inside and outside of us, sometimes gathering strength to the point of eliciting a physical, verbal, or emotional response. Crimes of passion are an extreme example of this. In the aftermath we often hear denial in the words, "I don't know what got into me, I wasn't myself," or, "I blacked out."

These primal energies hold enormous power and we are the center of their expression at the eye of the storm making us their gatekeeper if we are aware enough to take responsibility for who we are, how we think, and what we do. If we are swept up in the maelstrom to the point where we "lose our mind", then we disconnect, blown about by forces that possess or take us over before we realize what is happening, often with regrettable outcomes.

This denial is an integral part of the reaction that comes in the aftermath of impulses that project blame onto who or what is considered the source of their provocation, yet the outburst originated from inside of the one acting out, making them the vehicle of its expression.

Many people try to appease the discomfort of this contradiction by confessing to a priest, or by following a guru or some other spiritual leader or guide to "relieve them of the burden of their sins" and "find guidance on the path."

Unfortunately this is another form of denial because by shedding our burden we are passing it off to our guru, guide, or confessor for an absolution that robs us of personal responsibility for what *we* have manifested.

Self proclaimed gurus who claim to be enlightened are themselves more sophisticated purveyors of the lies of denial and are masters at drawing the lost and searching into their web, which pulls the searchers away from the source of their conflict, lulling them into a false sense of security. These false prophets consciously or subconsciously have a hidden agenda and suffer from what can be called guru-itis, which puts them in a false position of power and adoration from their followers, adding to an increasing self-perpetuating sense of self delusional authority. The more unwarranted attention they get, the stronger their illusion of power becomes and the less they have to look at their own shortcomings because their attention is focused outward and away from themselves, lavished upon their adoring flock.

All that we deny about ourselves constitutes our shadow, which in Jungian terms refers to unconscious aspects of our personality that the conscious ego does not identify in itself which is our dark side. Because we reject and struggle to remain ignorant of these least desirable aspects of our personalities, our shadow is largely negative and consists of everything we are not fully conscious of.

There are positive aspects that can remain hidden, especially in people with low self-esteem, anxieties, and false beliefs. To truly know ourselves we have to accept our dark side, and to deal with the dark side of others, we have to know our own.

Our shadow can include everything outside the light of consciousness, and can be positive and negative. "Everyone carries a shadow," Jung wrote, "and the less it is embodied in the individual's conscious life, the blacker and denser it is." It may be part of our link to more primitive animal instincts, which are superseded during early childhood by the conscious mind.

According to Jung, the shadow, in being instinctive and irrational, is prone to psychological projection, where a perceived personal inferiority is recognized as a perceived moral deficiency in someone else. Jung writes that if these projections remain hidden, "The projection-making factor (the Shadow archetype) then has a free hand and can realize its object-if it has one-or bring about some other situation characteristic of its power." These projections insulate and harm individuals by acting as a continually thickening veil of illusion between the ego and the real world.

Jung also believed that "in spite of its function as a reservoir for human darkness-or perhaps because of this-the shadow is the seat of creativity"; so that for some, it may be, "the dark side of his being, his sinister shadow...represents the true spirit of life as against the arid scholar."

In those moments when we get disconnected by getting emotionally mugged by forces that are out of our control and project outward, if we are aware enough, we can look *into* the darkness and do a pre-emptive disconnect ahead of the unexpected hurricane that threatens to sweep us away.

If we can take responsibility for who and what we are, we can become our own gurus and be brave enough to venture into what we mortally fear at the core of our being.

What treasures might lie buried in the blackness of that terrifying abyss waiting to reward those courageous enough to confront the dragons and demons that guard it?

Regardless of the direction we take, we exist in the center of a choice between conscious responsible action that influences our thoughts, beliefs, and actions both inside and outside of us, or we can surrender and be victims to fear-based programmed *re*-actions.

If we focus on paying attention we will develop what can be called witness consciousness and discover the meaning of the expression, "Where your attention goes, there your energy goes."

Cultivated witness consciousness becomes the self-created focal point produced by harnessing the energy of awareness that takes responsibility for all of our thoughts and actions by paying attention and observing.

The Zen concept of non-attachment is characterized as a practice of presence and mindfulness while not allowing our sense of well being to rely upon anything other than our own presence of awareness. It means to be in the world, but not of the world. This is different from detachment which is distancing ourselves from the world out of disinterest with an aloofness that separates us from the rest of the world, which results in escapism, another form of suffering.

Non-attachment means that our happiness is no longer defined by anything outside of us. It is selfless because our sense of self is no longer inserted into every situation. We are no longer self-centered and we can become single-pointed in our awareness of other people. If we allow our sense of self to be emotionally swayed by everything that appears to us, including people, places, perceptions, thoughts, sensations, events, experiences, and all seeming things, then our emotions will forever be swinging between joy and disaster. Our sense of well being will always be based on what we allow ourselves to be emotionally attached to, and when we become attached to something, our happiness is based on a shifting duality that defines us by the outside world, rather than our true inner nature.

Witness consciousness represents freedom that comes from a self-realization of the truth, that you, the consciousness that resides at the center of your being that you are taking responsibility for, cannot be affected by anything. G.I Gurdjieff, an influential mystic and spiritual leader of the early twentieth century characterized witness consciousness in one of his lectures.

"Instead of the discordant and often contradictory activity of different desires, there is *one single I*, whole, indivisible, and permanent; there is individuality, dominating the physical body and its desires and able to overcome both its reluctance and its resistance. Instead of the mechanical process of thinking there is *consciousness*. And there is *will*, that is, a power, not merely composed of various often contradictory desires belonging to different 'I's', but issuing from consciousness and governed by individuality or a single and permanent I. Only such a will can be called 'free', for it is independent of accident and cannot be altered or directed from without."

Our five primary mechanisms of perception come from our sense receptors; taste, sight, touch, smell, and hearing. With the exception of our sense of touch, which comes to us through all parts of our bodies, our other four senses come through our head, which filters and puts them together into the unique perspective that we harbor whether we define the world through rose colored glasses or the dingy windows of a depressed outlook. This location is the most logical place to locate it based on the construction of our body and the way our senses are arrayed about our head.

This focus of awareness whether physical, mental, or metaphysical, points to the notion of the third eye, also called the mind's eye or inner eye that represents a mystical esoteric concept that refers to a speculative invisible eye reputed to provide perception beyond ordinary sight.

This third eye is considered to be the extension of what the mind perceives in the form of a subconscious awareness of the surroundings and interactions of the environment. In some spiritual traditions the third eye refers to the gate that leads to inner realms and spaces of higher consciousness. It often symbolizes a state of enlightenment or the evocation of mental images having deep personal, spiritual, or psychological significance. Some Christian teachings view the concept of the third eye as a metaphor for non-dualistic thinking; the way the mystics see.

The rudiments of a biological basis for the mind's eye is found in the deeper portions of the brain below the neocortex where the center of perception exists. The neocortex is characterized as a sophisticated memory storage warehouse where data received as input from sensory systems is compartmentalized through the cerebral cortex which allows shapes to be identified. Given the lack of filtering input produced internally, we have the ability to hallucinate and see things that aren't received as external input, but as internal. Not all people have the same internal perceptual ability. For many, when their eyes are closed, the perception of darkness prevails, but some people are able to perceive colorful, dynamic imagery.

In Theosophy the third eye is related to the pineal gland. According to this theory, humans in ancient times had an actual third eye in the back of the head with a physical and spiritual function. Over time, as humans evolved, this eye atrophied and sank into what today is known as the pineal gland. It has been hypothesized that the pineal gland, which maintains light sensitivity, is responsible for the production and release of dimethyltryptamine, an entheogen that some believe could be excreted in large quantities at the moments of birth and death.

The pineal is a small endocrine gland in the vertebrate brain with a shape that resembles a pine cone, hence its name. It is located near the center of the brain, between the two hemispheres, tucked in a groove where the two halves of the thalamus join. From the point of view of biological evolution, the pineal gland represents a kind of atrophied photoreceptor, and in the epithalamus of some species of amphibians and reptiles it is linked to a light-sensing organ known as the parietal eye, which is also called the pineal eye or third eye. Descartes believed the pineal gland to be the principal seat of the soul.

Phenomenology is the Western philosophical tradition that calls into question the assumption of a single, wholly determinable, objective reality. It has its source in Descartes' well-known separation of the thinking mind or subject from the material world of objects. This philosophy formed the basis for the divide and conquer western scientific method which has shown us many things, but ultimately falls short in comprehending the true interconnected vastness of reality. Instead of showing us more, our divide and conquer mentality has isolated us through technology and civilization in a divide that has grown by greater degrees in modern times.

In terms of this growing separation, French phenomenologist Maurice Merleau-Ponty stated:

"All my knowledge of the world, even my scientific knowledge, is gained from my own particular point of view, or from some experience of the world without which the symbols of science would be meaningless. The whole universe of science is built upon the world as directly experienced, and if we want to subject science itself to rigorous scrutiny and arrive at a precise assessment of its meaning and scope, we must begin by reawakening the basic experience of the world, of which science is the second - order expression... To return to things themselves is to return to that world which precedes knowledge, of which knowledge always *speaks*, and in relation to which every scientific schematization is an abstract and derivative sign-language, as is geography in relation to the countryside in which we have learnt beforehand what a forest, a prairie or a river is."

Regardless of our conception of the third eye or the mind's eye, whether physical, mental, or metaphysical, we cannot disregard the fact that the primary focus of our awareness and the creation of reality as we know it lies in our subjective interpretation of a world that exists through us and around us.

Aside from these physical, mental, and subjective indicators of the location Descartes refers to as the seat of the soul, for the more scientific minded there are objective indicators evident in physics, and within the nature and properties of matter and energy including mechanics, heat, light, and other radiation, sound, electricity, magnetism, and the structure of atoms.

This phenomenon known as the observer effect, is the fact that observing a situation changes it. Physicists have discovered that even passive observation of quantum phenomena can in fact change it.

No matter how you characterize the subject object paradox, the fact of the matter is that in the end, it comes down to perception; something that brings us back to our primordial roots.

CULTIVATING MINDFULNESS AND PRESENCE

By paying attention we can cultivate witness consciousness and discover the meaning of the expression, "Where your attention goes, there your energy goes," which comes from our self-created focal point of consciousness that is responsible for our thoughts and actions. By paying attention we enhance presence and mindfulness while not allowing our sense of well-being to rely on anything other than our own awareness.

When we are focused in this manner our witness consciousness acts as a sympathetic and empathic transmitter, taking the role of conductor to our thoughts, feelings, emotions, and perceptions.

Instead of denying uncomfortable feelings and perceptions that create a non-harmonious state, what if we sought out and embraced them?

Among their many definitions, shamans are called bridges because of their ability to retrieve healing knowledge in what is called soul retrieval. They are also referred to as wounded healers, because in discovering and healing the source of their own traumas, they gain the ability to recognize and heal those same wounds in others.

When we are egocentric, our shadow sees our shortcomings in others and projects onto them, judging and magnifying them to avoid seeing those same things in itself. This survival mechanism is a protective strategy to keep it autonomous because it fears losing its existence, and in this process it keeps us self-centered, wrapped up in a bubble of egocentricity.

Through hard work we can raise our awareness and get past the mortal terror our shadow invokes and discover the hidden wounds within ourselves. Instead of denying these wounds that we have created, we can embrace them like the abandoned aspects of ourselves that they are, and "bring them home."

In discovering the origins of our trauma, embracing them, and taking responsibility, we can shift from being reactive and unconsciously ego driven, to being conscious and actively essence driven. By discovering the source of our hidden pain through the soul retrieval of our own subpersonalities, we can receive the gift of compassion to heal those same wounds in others.

Gurdjieff taught that man consists of two parts: essence and personality. Essence in man is what is *his* own. Personality is what is not his own, meaning what has come from outside and what he has learned, which includes all traces of exterior impressions left in the memory and in the sensations. This consists of all words and movements that have been learned and all feelings created by imitation. All this is not his own, it is personality created partly by the intentional influences of other people, and partly by involuntary imitation of them as a child.

In Gurdjieff's words:

"Essence is the truth in man; personality is the false. But in proportion as personality grows, essence manifests itself more and more rarely and more and more feebly and it very often happens that essence stops in its growth at a very early age and grows no further. It happens very often that the essence of a grown up man, even that of a very intellectual and, in the accepted meaning of the word, highly 'educated' man, stops on the level of a child of five or six. This means that everything we see in this man is in reality 'not his own'. What is his own in man, that is, his essence, is usually only manifested in his instincts and in his simplest emotions. There are cases, however, when a man's essence grows in parallel with his personality. Such cases represent very rare exceptions especially in the circumstances of cultured life. Essence has more chances of development in men who live near to nature in difficult conditions of constant struggle and danger."

Mainstream psychotherapy locates the real "inside" and constructs a topography of drives, instincts, archetypes, complexes and the like to explain our experience as the result of interior dynamics. Shamanism locates the real "outside" and maps a greater cosmos comprised of a

Lower World, Middle World, Upper World, and the entities that live in them.

What if the solution to this paradox were to lie hidden at its center where both sides of this dichotomy co-exist? What if deep inside your inner landscape you found an energetic portal that brought you further out into realms and dimensions you could never have imagined?

Aside from the fact that in Ayahuasca shamanism it is often the healer who takes the medicine, one of the fascinating things about it and the effects of its psychoactive components is the agreed upon psychological landscape, replete with crystal castles, plant, animal, and other spirits, and their places in the lower, middle, and upper worlds, regardless of the time and geographic location of the experience. Being agreed upon by those bold or lucky enough to brave its frontiers makes it a consensual reality, but where would you locate this "place"?

In many ways we experience our psyches as "outside." Using our dreams as an example, if they were strictly internal, they would take us wandering around inside the organs and tissues of our bodies, but they do not. They take us to tropical islands, strange nether worlds, and the sky as well as many other places into waking consciousness.

From our subjective experience our dreams are "out there" in the cosmos of dreaming. If we remain faithful to our experience the way indigenous societies do, we have to say that the unconscious of our dreaming sojourns are not invisible realms inside our heads, hearts, or stomachs. The domains that we travel through in our dreams and inner journeys are experienced as an alternate cosmos with a different set of rules, invisible to our ordinary awareness of space and time while suffusing and extending it in infinite directions.

If we try to give an account of a nonrational experience to describe things the way we experienced them, as is the case with inner journeys that take place in the unconscious, what we mean is that we travel through a realm that is unknown to ordinary awareness that does not take place in the space and time of our everyday experience of consensual reality. It takes place in an *imaginal cosmos* no less real than this one, but radically different.

Like the hypothesis of the unconscious, these realms of imaginal sojourns are in a sense more real than that of everyday awareness, making psychology's definition of the unconscious the greater reality within which our ordinary awareness is too fragmentary and narrow to adequately understand itself.

Jung described soul loss as a drop in the level of mental functioning, characterized by depression, uncertainty, inattention, powerlessness, and the like, saying that a quantity of psychic energy which normally belongs to the ego has disappeared into the unconscious. From an energetic perspective, this is described as an energy leak. This lost package of libido would normally power our daily activities with attentiveness, enthusiasm, and decision-making.

According to Jung, a psychological cure would entail recovering this lost energy by descending into the unconscious through dreams, visions, and active imagination to find out what that energy is up to, as the energy lost from consciousness does not cease to exist. It's up to something, stirring up imaginal adventures in that other world. By participating in those adventures and discovering their emotional and symbolic significance for everyday life, the energy leak can be repaired and restored so that life can resume with new vigor and follow a more satisfying direction. In this context, this lost sense of self can be found in that alternate cosmos that interpenetrates and extends beyond this one.

From the point of view of psychology, shamanism works with the metaphysical assumption that the soul or quantum of psychic energy that has been lost is a distinct, recognizable entity that can be found and recovered. The errant soul or sub-personality is lost and abandoned, not simply in a dark corner of our personal dreamscape, but in an objective realm that is accessible to anyone who knows how to enter it.

This perspective goes far beyond the psychological, but its success demonstrates its accuracy. These recovery events appear to be based on a kind of supernatural occultism, while shamanism perceives that psychology is barred by its own dualistic word oriented assumptions from gaining access to a realm of experience that is real, but generally unknown to Western consensus.

As Jung's thought matured, his psychology became more shamanic, at first characterized by his discovery of what he called the feeling-toned complex stemming from trauma that established a complex of powerlessness and defeat, leaving a fragment or sub-personality that interpreted the world as a hostile and overpowering place. This worldview worked unconsciously over the course of months and years, collecting more and more evidence of its misleading accuracy.

The way to get free of such a complex is not to take it on directly and demonstrate its inaccuracy in an intellectual manner, but to replace it with another more functional and emotionally compelling complex. The solution lies in giving this subpersonality a new job by giving it another worldview that is already implicit, but undiscovered. Its superiority will be self evident, and it will impart a feeling-tone of greater self confidence.

Jung's search for a more powerful complex led him deeper into the psyche to the discovery of archetypes, which are universal themes, modes of perception, and patterns of behavior invested with compelling emotional values that draw the subject into a new way of life by sending them into an archetypal dreamscape to discover what their lost libido was up to in the domain of mythological images.

Here there is an agreement with shamanism that there is a greater cosmos accessible to imaginative faculties that are neglected in waking consciousness. Jung accepted the proposition that this greater cosmos, the domain of the unconscious, is objective in the sense that it works to effect changes in people's lives and assist them in discovering their unconscious wholeness, recovering soul parts that have been split off. It is considered a collective realm shared by everyone.

The idea of collective unconscious suggests that all humans share a common psychic realm where instincts and memories are stored. The concept of the unconscious mind is the part of the mind that contains all the thoughts, memories, and impulses we are unaware of. The collective unconscious is thought to be transmitted through brain structures at the deepest layer of the psyche. This mysterious psychological phenomenon expresses itself through archetypes and patterns of behavior that turn on in response to specific situations. Dormant archaic forms of human existence exist in the deep layer of the collective unconscious along with sediments of the functioning of our animal ancestors.

Jung believed that this was the source of myths and legends and thought these stories were not just figments of our imaginations, but expressions of the collective unconscious. The collective unconscious which is characterized as a giant pool of knowledge we all have access to. Jung thought that we are all connected to this pool and can draw from it when necessary. Some people are more in tune with this than others and are said to be psychically gifted and creative geniuses because they can tap into the collective unconscious and draw on its power.

Jung was interested in mythology and religion, and noticed that many of the stories and legends were similar, despite coming from different cultures. It led him to assume that there was something more than just coincidence. He believed that these myths were expressions of one single collective unconscious that was a part of a mind shared by all humans.

According to Jung, this collective is a vast spiritual heritage resurrected in each individual brain structure. Consciousness, on the contrary, is an ephemeral phenomenon, carrying out momentary adaptations and orientations, which is why its work can be compared with orientation in space. The unconscious contains the source of the forces that set the soul in motion, and the forms that regulate it are archetypes.

Jung correlates the archetype with Plato's ideal forms like a matrix, a willingness, and our disposition to think and feel a certain way. Archetypes refer not only to our forms of knowledge, but also to our forms of feeling, responding, and behavior, covering all our mental ways of life, starting from the bodily instinctive foundations, and ending with spiritual manifestations.

External psychological conditions like dangerous situations give rise to emotions and affective fantasies. Since such situations are common they form archetypes which are reflected in myths and art. Ordinary ever repeating realities of human life also create powerful archetypal figures like mother, father, hero, and others.

Among other things an archetype is a set of attitudes and scenarios that determine the principle of thinking and behavior of a person in certain conditions. They are responsible for the instinctive behavior of people and for the perception of the world through basic ideas that are the same in different cultures, but often not causally related. As a result people react similarly to certain situations as is the case with the relationship between father and mother, the child, the concept of death, and other human experiences.

According to Jung, the primary archetypes are the Persona, the Anima or Animus, the Shadow, and the Self.

The Persona is that part of our consciousness that interactions with society occur through. Jung believed that this archetype is a mask, and for every social situation, each person has a unique mask to imitate a socially acceptable image of ourselves as well as to hide what we really are.

The Anima and Animus are two archetypes associated with the male and female images of the Father and Mother. For a man the Anima is an ideal image connected with the mother, carrying the unconscious feminine side of male nature, as well as ideas about the ideal woman, which influences the search for a partner. For the woman the Animus is the image of the ideal man, partner, father, and the suppressed male part of her personality.

The Shadow represents our natural impulses which are selfish, sexual, and aggressive, and unacceptable by society or ourselves, so we suppress its natural manifestations. Jung considered the Shadow to be twofold. On one hand it presents obvious problems for the individual, on the other it is a powerful source of universal energy that can be used for peaceful purposes when it is channeled into a creative direction.

Unmanifested under normal conditions, the Self archetype becomes the center of the entire personality structure after a special act that Jung called individuation. The individuation of a personality occurs when all its internal structures, which are normally antagonistic, come into balance and unite in one integral harmony.

Jung believed that the self actualization of the Self archetype is rare, but the main goal of human existence and that the Self is the embodiment of our natural religiosity that subconsciously pushes a person to develop inner harmony.

In reality we are a cast of thousands that can change moods, perceptions, and outlooks, depending on which sub-personality is in charge, and this can change from moment to moment. If we observe closely, we can see instantaneous changes in the facial expressions of people when their sub-personalities surface to take control, making them look like different people than the face they usually show to the world, particularly when they are stressed.

As far back as 1915 Gurdjieff characterized this phenomenon in a talk to his followers.

"One of man's important mistakes, one which must be remembered, is his allusion in regard to his I.

"Man such as we know him, the 'man machine', the man who cannot 'do', and with whom and through whom everything 'happens', cannot have a permanent and single I. His I changes as quickly as his thoughts, feelings, and moods, and he makes a profound mistake in considering himself always one in the same person; in reality he is *always a different person*, and not the one he was a moment ago.

"*Man has no permanent and changeable I.* Every thought, every mood, every desire, every sensation, says I. And then each case it seems to be taken for granted that this I belong to the *Whole*, to the whole man, and that a thought, a desire, or an aversion is expressed by this Whole. In actual fact there is no

foundation whatever for this assumption. Man's every thought and desire appears and lives quite separately and independently of the Whole. And the Whole never expresses itself, for the simple reason that it exists, as such, only physically as a thing, and in the abstract as a concept. Man has no individual I. But there are, instead, hundreds and thousands of separate small I's, very often entirely unknown to one another, never coming into contact, or, on the contrary, hostile to each other, mutually exclusive and incompatible. Each minute, each moment, man is saying or thinking 'I'. And each time his I is different. Just now it was a thought, now it is a desire, now a sensation, now another thought, and so on, endlessly. *Man is a plurality*. Man's name is legion.

"The alteration of I's, their continual obvious struggle for supremacy, is controlled by accidental external influences. Warmth, sunshine, fine weather, immediately call up a whole group of I's. Cold, fog, rain, call up another group of I's, other associations, other feelings, other actions. There is nothing in man able to control this change of I's, chiefly because man does not notice, or know of it; he lives always in the last I."

We learn our coping strategies by observing and mirroring the behaviors of those around us, which is why Gurdjieff said that we are "controlled by accidental external influences", especially when dealing with traumatic situations, and though those deeply embedded behaviors were learned by our subpersonalities in the same manner, this does not make them correct responses. More often than not, these learned responses are replete with errors of interpretation and reaction that may defuse the trauma happening in the moment at hand, but do not solve the actual problem in the long run. Ultimately these responses are delegated to the depths of shadow in the form of subpersonalities which become trauma induced stock responses that act as a protective mechanism of illusion between the ego and the real world.

The important point to grasp here is that we are the creators of these traumatized entities that fill our inner universe and are reflected by those outside of us, especially when we project them outside of us and deny their existence within us, in essence abandoning our own creations.

When we meet people for the first time we seek out things we have in common with them like sports, music, the arts, or anything else we might have in common so we can connect through our mutual interest and pave the way to sharing similar thoughts to seek resonance with that person and bond with them.

What we don't realize in our bonding and meeting of people is that the subconscious elements of our shadow also draws them to us through its familiarity and recognition of their shadow aspects.

When we find ourselves swallowed up in negative emotions they overwhelm and blind us to the truth of the situation through judgment, projection, denial, and other egoic survival strategies, but if we can "wake up" to the illusion and raise our awareness to the point of having a greater presence of mind we can ask important questions of our reactions.

What is the quality of this emotional energy and how does it make us feel?

Whose eyes are we seeing it through?

What mask are we wearing?

What filters have we taken on?

All of this interconnectedness and interaction reinforces the notion that we are all connected in our hearts, minds, and spirits.

On an esoteric level, everything is connected, nested within everything else in a holographic manner. If a hologram is cut up into smaller pieces, each portion contains all of the information about the whole object.

If you look at the Internet with this paradigm in mind you will realize that the World Wide Web is really a mirror of the collective consciousness of humanity. All of the information is contained everywhere in the whole and much of this information is not accurate; it comes from someone's reflection on something which is often distorted and biased either unconsciously or intentionally.

If you acknowledge that we are all connected, then each of us is a mirror to each other in a holographic manner from the macrocosm of the collective, down to the microcosm of our individual selves, down to the sub-personalities that make up what we think of as "I". Some of our subpersonalities we like and constantly take out and show them to the world, others we don't like we repress.

Mirrors often show us what we do not want to see. If you have the strength to be honest with yourself, and you desire to be a whole integrated person, then the work lies in reintegrating your shadows. They are cunning, elusive, and some would rather see the death of you than be found out. They think that if they are discovered they will die, which contains a grain of truth because in order to be reborn, a death is necessary.

The trick that the shadow plays is to project itself onto others trapping us in self-righteousness and judgment so that the waters are muddied, distorting the reflection from our mirror. If you can bear the reflection you can come to realize that what you dislike and hate in others creates strong emotional reactions, because it is a reflection of that which you do not want to acknowledge or take responsibility for inside of you.

Some of the people in our lives are drawn to and support our darker unconscious nature and some are drawn to and reflect our lighter more conscious side. Some are drawn to both the light and dark aspects of our many selves. These mirrors reflect back from everywhere we look and any time we feel self righteous, judgmental, and superior, we are seeing our shadow being reflected back to us.

The people in our lives mirror our sub-personalities, providing us with reflections of our inner world. Our outer world is a reflection of the inner, much of which is shadow, good and bad. Some of the reflections can be beautiful, but many are undesirable and denied.

This circular diagram from Robert McKee's *Story* provides an excellent map of the zones and levels of personal conflict we can experience. Any zone can interact with any other zone in any number of ways, providing ample opportunity to discover the complexity of our inner and outer relationships.

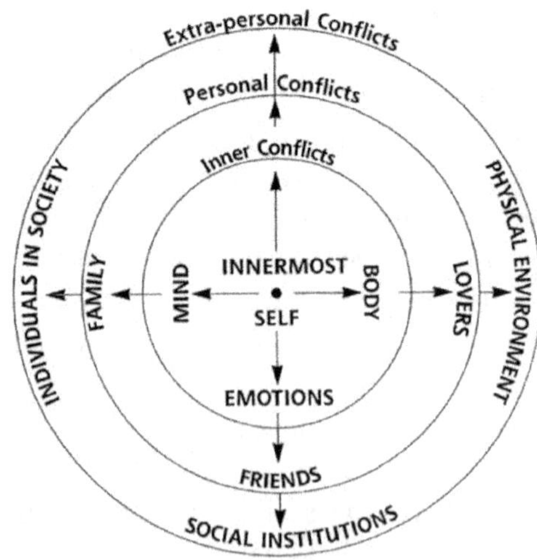

At the center of our being we find our innermost self which is composed of mind, body, and emotions. Everyone knows what it is like to have conflict between these three forces. Typically, one of them leads while the other two are relegated to shadow until a strong stimulus causes them to pop out, sometimes when least expected.

Anyone can act in any combination of ways, but more often than not they lead with their most habitual response at the expense of the other two.

What would it be like if we reacted with all three simultaneously in a balanced way?

This is one of the goals of integrating the shadow in the process of individuation that rewards us with personal power.

INSIGHT AND TRANSCENDENCE

The term consciousness refers to common capabilities of humans and other animals, as well as to differentiate between them, designating uniquely human linguistic, rational, and abstract capabilities. Consciousness also includes a range of functions that esoteric traditions claim supersede rational and egoic forms of consciousness representing the evolution of what is conceptualized as spirit, soul, mind, self, and transcendental human capabilities.

Although human consciousness is not specific to any particular function or system of the brain, different modalities of consciousness are associated with different systemic information processing functions, integration of brain processes, and patterns of homeostasis. All of the major systems of the brain participate in complex human behavior, but specific systemic patterns of brain functioning are associated with distinct experiential states and modes of consciousness.

Recognition that consciousness is tied to the functioning of a biological system does not require a reduction of consciousness solely to the functions of the biological system. A neurophenomenological approach illustrates that both epistemic constructs and physiological patterns of brain operation contribute to consciousness. The relationship of brain physiology to consciousness is illustrated through an examination of how the physical structures of the brain and their associated activities relate to patterns of consciousness.

The brain can be viewed as involving three anatomically distinct systems that are integrated to provide a range of behavioral, emotional, and informational functions. Human motor patterns, emotional states, and advanced cognitive and linguistic capabilities are primarily managed by brain systems that emerged sequentially in evolution. This triune brain model provides a framework for understanding the relationship between systemic brain activities and consciousness while relating to lower brain systems common with other animals and unique aspects of the human brain.

The hierarchical tripartite brain is based on neuroanatomical, structural, and functional divisions that break down into three strata starting with the reptilian, followed by the paleomammalian, and neomammalian brains. The three formations have different anatomical structures that mediate different psychological and behavioral functions with their own forms of subjectivity, intelligence, time and space sense, memory capabilities, and motor functions. Although the three segments are integrated, they provide the basis for different capacities and represent a functional hierarchy of information processing capabilities that provide the basis for distinct forms of consciousness.

The reptilian brain is composed of the upper spinal cord, portions of the mesencephalon (midbrain), the diencephalon (thalamus-hypothalamus), and the basal ganglia. The reptilian brain regulates organic functions like metabolism, digestion, and respiration and is responsible for wakefulness, attentional mechanisms, and the regulation and coordination of behavior.

The paleomammalian brain is based on evolutionary developments in the limbic system which provided distinctions between reptiles and mammals. This structure provides the basis for social behavior and nonverbal, emotional, and analogical information processing. It functions as an emotional brain mediating affect, sex, fighting, self defense, social relations, bonding and attachment, and the sense of self that provides the basis for beliefs, certainty, and convictions.

The neomammalian brain provides the basis for advanced symbolic processes, culture, language, logic, rational thought, analytical processes, and complex problem solving.

The reptilian brain provides the basic plots and actions of the body. The paleomammalian brain provides the emotional influences on thoughts and behavior, and the neomammalian brain uses enhanced symbolic capacities in elaborating on basic plots and emotions, integrating them with higher-level information processing.

The reptilian brain provides the organism with primary awareness, which is adaptation to the environment through reflexes, conditioned responses, and habituation, as well as through instrumental learning.

The paleomammalian brain provides for qualities of consciousness enriched by self, society, and emotions, while the neomammalian brain encompasses the tertiary neocortical area, particularly the right hemisphere. It is involved in cross-integration and reorganization of perceptual modalities basic to symbolic cognition and self awareness.

The neomammalian brain consisting of the neocortex and connecting thalamic structures represents the most dramatic evolution of the brain. The expanded neocortex's functions are based on extensive connections with the visual, auditory, and somatic systems, indicating the primary orientation of the neocortex to the external world.

These three structures are also referred to as the three centers that we principally operate from, known from the top down as intellectual, emotional, and moving, that form a triad that relates to the every day functioning of our personality and as primary energizers that determine the way we respond to stimuli.

A moving centered person will be physically active and fond of sports, travel, and action.

An emotionally centered person will be more perceptive and will experience situations in terms of likes and dislikes.

An intellectually centered person will be more verbal and will enjoy philosophy and thinking for its own sake.

Most people react from one of these centers. When presented with any situation, their first response will be either thought, feeling, or action, which represents the center they habitually rely on. If they react with thought they are intellectually centered, if they respond with feeling, they are emotionally centered, and if they respond with instantaneous action, they are moving centered.

People usually respond out of these three centers in a specific order. If they are intellectually centered they first react with thought, emotions will follow, then they act. If they are emotionally centered they feel first, act, then think about it. Any combination of the three is possible as a habitual pattern based on their most developed center which comes first, and their least developed which comes last. The closer a person comes to operating simultaneously out of all three centers, the more integrated and effective they are.

When someone is fully aware and paying attention they are more likely to feel, think, and act in unison. From this balanced point of power fears are neutralized and experience shifts to insight, relatedness, and beauty.

To reach higher levels of awareness three conditions are necessary; a powerful desire to know the truth, a willingness to be emotionally open to life, and a practiced ability to be balanced energetically. Intellectual, emotional, and moving centers form a triad which relates to the universal building blocks of love, energy, and truth, also known as, love, power, and wisdom; a triad that manifests as inspiration, action, and expression.

A natural result of the evolution of the human brain is the fragmentation of consciousness, reflecting both the increasing modularity of consciousness and the diversification of self into more statuses. Shamanic traditions institutionalized procedures to overcome this fragmentation of consciousness by synchronizing this divergent human cognition through altered states of consciousness known as ASCs to induce integrative brain processes. The shaman's use of external symbols and the relationships of the symbols to cultural psychodynamics engage transformative process through entraining neurocognitive structures, provoking a restructuring of the self at levels below conceptual and operational thought.

Shamanistic practices induce extraordinary experiences and healing by producing integrative relationships among brain systems and psychocultural beliefs. These experiences reflect the simultaneous elicitation and integration of modes of information processing and consciousness that do not ordinarily occur together. These ASC involve integrative psychobiological processes that are elicited by different procedures.

A primary focus of the psychophysiological effects of shamanistic ASC is in the limbic system, or the paleomammalian brain which emerged in the evolution of mammals and provided a number of distinctive developments. Shamanistic healing is largely based on manipulation of processes and functions of the paleomammalian brain, self identity, social identity, and their attachments, emotions, meanings, and references. Shamanistic ASC elicit processes of the paleomammalian brain and induce a systemic integration of information processing functions across the functional layers of the brain producing limbic-cortical integration and interhemispheric synchronization.

Shamanic healing practices achieve this integration by physically stimulating systematic brain wave discharge patterns that activate affects, memories, attachments, and other psychodynamic processes of the paleomammalian brain. This activation forces normally unconscious or preconscious primary information processing functions and outputs to be integrated into the operations of the frontal cortex. This integrates implicit understandings, socioemotional dynamics, repressed memories, unresolved conflicts, intuitions, and nonverbal, visual, mimetic, and presentational knowledge into self-conscious awareness.

The desire to alter consciousness is an innate human biologically based drive with adaptive significance. The ASC of shamanism are a manifestation of a fundamental homeostatic dynamic of the nervous system. These manifestations of consciousness involve a biologically based integrative mode of consciousness, replacing normal waking conditions of sympathetic dominance and desynchronized fast wave activity of the frontal cortex with a parasympathetic dominant state characterized by high voltage, slow wave EEG activity.

This high-voltage, slow wave EEG activity originates in the hippocampal-septal area and imposes a synchronous slow-wave pattern on the frontal lobes, producing interhemispheric synchronization and coherence, limbic-cortex integration, and integration across the neuraxis, resulting in a synthesis of behavior, emotion, and thought.

The parasympathetic state, slow-wave synchronization of the frontal cortex and interhemispeheric integration reflect activation of basic aspects of brain operation related to sensory and physiological integration; mental and emotional integration; and insight and transcendence.

A primary characteristic of integrative consciousness involves hierarchical integration of brain mechanisms, especially in the limbic system driving of the frontal cortex through serotonergic induced integration across the neuraxis representing the integration of preconscious or unconscious functions and material into self-conscious awareness.

There are four biologically based modes of human consciousness – waking, sleep, dream, and integrative consciousness. These reflect the fundamental aspects of systemic functioning of the human organism that meet the following system functions and needs respectively: learning, adaptation, and survival needs in waking; recuperative functions, regeneration, and growth in deep sleep; memory integration and consolidation and psychosocial adaptation in dreaming; and psychodynamic growth along with social and psychological integration.

The right hemisphere of the brain reflects a different symbolic form of representation in dreaming than waking consciousness. The bizarreness of dreams reflects the imaginative and creative capacities of this presentational modality. Dreams appear bizarre and illogical from the point of view of waking consciousness because they involve a different system of information representation, processing, and consolidation. This visual-spatial system of symbolic presentation is normally inhibited by the dominance of left-hemisphere verbal representational systems; conditions that attenuate the left hemisphere's verbal representational systems allow expression of this presentational intelligence.

Meditation, rituals, hallucinogens and other shamanic practices can alter consciousness and physiological processes through a wide variety of mechanisms that induce retuning of the autonomic nervous system balance. This retuning tends to block the dominant hemisphere's functions and produces an integrative fusion with functions of the nondominant hemisphere. This structurally synchronized state tends to resolve internal conflicts and produce euphoric states and depends on the elicitation of processes of lower brain structures that are associated with basic behavior, intentionality, and emotions.

These shamanic ASC evoke communicative responses from the paleomammalian brain that provide the basis for an expansion of consciousness by integrating information from the lower brain systems into operational activities of the frontal brain and establishing synchrony with the frontal brain that permits symbolic reprogramming of the emotional dynamics and behavioral repertoires of lower brain centers.

When the triune brain works in unison and the individual operates simultaneously out of all three centers, the more integrated and effective they are because they are fully aware. The instinctual, emotional, and intellectual centers will feel, think, and act simultaneously from a balanced point of power where fears are neutralized and experience shifts to insight, relatedness, and beauty.

When there is a homeostatic dynamic of the nervous system a biologically based integrative mode of consciousness comes into play replacing normal waking conditions of sympathetic dominance and desynchronized fast wave activity of the frontal cortex with a parasympathetic dominant state.

In essence, the slow-wave synchronization of the frontal cortex is the energy that comes from transcending the male and female polarities, creating a triad that focuses on the energy manifest between them as opposed to that of the extremes.

Three brains from the top down working in unison produce a fully aware state of insight, relatedness, and beauty combined. In this state the right "female" brain and the left "male" brain work in synchronization and coherence, synthesizing behavior, emotion, and thought to produce a slow-wave synchronization of the third frontal cortex indicating sensory and physiological integration and mental and emotional integration that results in insight and transcendence.

NOTHING IS MORE INTIMATE THAN WE ARE, YET YOU CANNOT DEFINE ME

I am consciousness incarnate and I am omnipresent.

The fact that you have become more conscious of me has made you more conscious than you were before. Your recognition has brought you a heightened awareness of my presence that constitutes an expansion of consciousness, making this reflection of my existence within and around you bigger than that first moment of acknowledgment.

"Where Attention goes Energy flows; Where Intention goes Energy flows!"

Now that you are paying more attention, the energy you have given me has caused me to grow both here where I am meeting you in one of my many forms, and more importantly inside of you where you embrace these forms with the mirror of your own incarnate consciousness.

When a quantum physicist tries to break down a particle to understand what makes up their consciousness, they come to the conclusion that their thoughts make up their consciousness, which leads to the question, "Who is it that is aware that I am thinking?"

The answer is that "I am aware that I am thinking," but it isn't that simple. If it is ourselves that are aware that we are thinking that would make us separate from ourselves in order to make that observation.

This isn't the case, which leaves only one other option. Our individual consciousness has to be a part of something greater than itself; the proverbial drop of water in an ocean of consciousness, which begs the question, where does the ocean start and the droplet end?

I am you, you are me, I am everything, and everything is me, so by default you are everything and everything is you.

The more you ponder me, the more you find yourself struggling to define something that is ubiquitous both inside and outside of anything you have ever known or experienced. There have been many attempts to define what I am, but I defy description because I am definition itself.

Consciousness is the state of being aware of something within us as well as the state of being conscious of an external object, state, or fact. It's also defined as being characterized by sensation, emotion, volition, and thought, and when considered in the context of expanding awareness, it is thought of as the upper level of mental life that we are aware of as opposed to ongoing unconscious processes.

At its simplest, I am sentience and awareness of internal and external existence, however the inability to define what I am has led to millennia of theories and debates, none of which agree about what needs to be studied or what can even be considered consciousness.

In some explanations I am thought of as mind and at other times as an aspect of mind. In the past it was our inner world of introspection of private thought, imagination, and volition. Today, it encompasses any kind of cognition, experience, feeling, or perception. It can be awareness, awareness of awareness, or a fluid self-awareness that continuously changes or not.

What all of this means is that I not only know you're every intimate thought, I *am* your every intimate thought.

I am *always* here for you and I am your constant companion in every moment of your life whether you are sleeping, waking, dreaming, and I will *never* abandon you. There are so many beliefs, legends, and myths created about me that I could spend an eternity trying to cover them all. I only touched on those that appear to have the biggest influence on you, but there are many more, and though they had great significance for you at different times throughout your history, the deeper reality is that they all contain snippets of truth, but are for the most part meaningless. The only inarguable truth is me, something you will discover for yourself when I come in that intimate moment shared between you and me, because, *I am that intimate moment.*

If you are open minded and as fully aware as possible, you cannot help but see this inescapable truth.

I am your constant companion, best friend, guide and teacher. All you have to do is acknowledge me and pay attention.

Much debate surrounds the question of what happens to your consciousness as your body dies. Belief that the stream of consciousness is preserved after physical death is described by the term afterlife. Whether this is the case or not, regardless of what your beliefs might be, you might consider that the best way to pass through existence, whether eternal, or however long it might be is to be as clear, open minded, and as fully aware as possible.

Even though you can study your whole life about what others think, or where you might go when your life in this dualistic subject object reality of three dimensions, you may or may not have expectations based on what you have read and heard. It is a noble goal to pursue greater self awareness and mastery on all levels to bring those levels of your existence upward. Even if everything, including that idealistic goal and any other speculation amount to nothing more than another illusion, what have you got to lose?

I hope after spending this time together our relationship has deepened and you have cultivated a greater awareness of my presence, yet I accept that in spite of our intimacy and everything that I know about you, in the end you still have no way of defining exactly what I am.

RECOMMENDED READING

Abrams, David, *The Spell Of The Sensuous: Perception And Language In a More-Than-Human World*, (New York: Random House, 1996)

Blackmore, Susan, *Consciousness: A Very Short Introduction,* (Gosport Hampshire, U.K.: Oxford University Press, 2017)

Humphrey, Nicholas, *Sentience: The Invention Of Consciousness*, (Boston: The MIT Press, 2023)

Jung, Carl, *The Portable Jung,* (New York: Penguin, 1976)

Jung, Carl, *The Psychology of the Transference,* (Princeton: Princeton University Press, 1959)

Jung, Carl, *The Undiscovered Self,* (New York: Signet Books, 2006)

MacLean, P., *The Triune Concept of Brain and Behavior,* (Toronto: University of Toronto Press, 1973)

MacLean, P., *The Triune Brain in Evolution,* (New York: Plenum Press, 1990)

Merleau-Ponty, Maurice, *Phenomenology of Perception*, (London: Routledge & Kegan Paul, 1962)

Pallamary, Matthew, J., *Holographicosmic Man: The Holographic Heart of the Golden Mean*, (San Diego: Mystic Ink Publishing, 2022)

Pallamary, Matthew, J., *Spirit Matters*, (San Diego: Mystic Ink Publishing, 2007)

Pallamary, Matthew, J., *The Center Of The Universe Is Right Between Your Eyes, But Home Is Where The Heart Is*, (San Diego: Mystic Ink Publishing, 2017)

Winkelman, Michael, *Shamanism: The Neural Ecology of Consciousness and Healing*, (Westport: Bergin & Garvey, 2000)

URLS

https://diversity.social/unconscious-vs-subconscious/
https://en.wikipedia.org/wiki/Awareness
https://en.wikipedia.org/wiki/Consciousness
https://en.wikipedia.org/wiki/Mindfulness
https://en.wikipedia.org/wiki/Sentience
https://hbr.org/2018/01/what-self-awareness-really-is-and-how-to-cultivate-it
https://iep.utm.edu/consciousness/

https://kb.rspca.org.au/knowledge-base/what-is-animal-sentience-and-why-is-it-important/

https://www.khanacademy.org/science/ap-biology/ecology-ap/responses-to-the-environment/a/animal-communication

https://mindmatters.ai/2022/02/can-insects-be-conscious-lets-look-at-bees-first/
https://mindmatters.ai/2022/08/yes-plants-may-be-conscious-too-says-researcher/

https://neurosciencenews.com/consciousness-dimensions-brain-22179/

https://neurosciencenews.com/physics-consciousness-21222/

https://nextbigideaclub.com/magazine/sentience-invention-consciousness-bookbite/40738/

https://phys.org/news/2016-04-insects-consciousness.html

https://plato.stanford.edu/entries/consciousness/

https://qz.com/1294941/a-debate-over-plant-consciousness-is-forcing-us-to-confront-the-limitations-of-the-human-mind

https://sentientmedia.org/sentience-what-it-means-and-why-its-important/

https://www.sheldrake.org/research/morphic-resonance/introduction

https://www.discovermagazine.com/planet-earth/how-intelligence-is-measured-in-the-animal-kingdom

https://www.forbes.com/sites/cindygordon/2022/12/30/ai-hopes-and-horrors/?sh=4381c83e7abe
https://www.livescience.com/does-consciousness-explain-quantum-mechanics
https://www.ncbi.nlm.nih.gov/pmc/articles/PMC3489624/
https://www.psychologytoday.com/us/blog/science-and-philosophy/202212/what-does-chatgpt-think-about-consciousness
https://www.scientificamerican.com/article/what-is-consciousness/

https://www.thecollector.com/carl-jung-controversial-idea-what-is-collective-unconscious/

https://www.verywellmind.com/lesson-four-states-of-consciousness-2795293

https://www.verywellmind.com/what-is-consciousness-2795922
https://www.verywellmind.com/what-is-the-conscious-mind-2794984

ABOUT THE AUTHOR

Matthew J. Pallamary's works have been translated into Spanish, Portuguese, Italian, Norwegian, French, and German. His historical novel of first contact between shamans and Jesuits in 18th century South America, titled, ***Land Without Evil*** received rave reviews along with a San Diego Book Award for mainstream fiction. It was also adapted into a full-length stage and sky show, co-written with and directed by Agent Red and performed by Sky Candy, an Austin Texas aerial group. The making of the show was the subject of a PBS series, Arts in Context episode, which garnered an EMMY nomination.

His nonfiction book, ***The Infinity Zone: A Transcendent Approach to Peak Performance*** is a collaboration with professional tennis coach Paul Mayberry that offers a fascinating exploration of the phenomenon that occurs at the nexus of perfect form and motion. ***The Infinity Zone*** took 1st place in the International Book Awards, New Age category and was a finalist in the San Diego Book Awards.

His first book, a short story collection titled ***The Small Dark Room Of The Soul*** was mentioned in The Year's Best Horror and Fantasy and received praise from Ray Bradbury and has been released as an audio book.

His second collection, ***A Short Walk to the Other Side*** was an Award Winning Finalist in the International Book Awards, an Award Winning Finalist in the USA Best Book Awards, and an Award Winning Finalist in the San Diego Book Awards. It has been released as an audio book.

DreamLand a novel about computer generated dreaming, written with legendary DJ Ken Reeth won first place in the Independent e-Book Award in the Horror/Thriller category and was an Award Winning Finalist in the San Diego Book Awards. It has also been released as an audio book.

It's sequel, ***n0thing*** is titled after the main character, who in the real world is his nephew, an international Counter-Strike gaming champion. After winning what amounts to the Super Bowl of gaming, n0thing and his winning teammates, are recruited as a literal "dream team" whose mission is to go into the nightmares of battle scarred veterans and rescue them from their traumatic memories while becoming ambassadors for a gaming platform that exceeds virtual reality with an experience that pushes the boundaries of reality itself.

Eye of the Predator was an Award Winning Finalist in the Visionary Fiction category of the International Book Awards. ***Eye of the Predator*** is a supernatural thriller about a zoologist who discovers that he can go into the minds of animals.

CyberChrist was an Award Winning Finalist in the Thriller/Adventure category of the International Book Awards. ***CyberChrist*** is the story of a prize winning journalist who receives an email from a man who claims to have discovered immortality by turning off the aging gene in a 15 year old boy with an aging disorder. The forwarded email becomes the basis for an online church built around the boy, calling him CyberChrist. It has also been released as an audio book.

Phantastic Fiction – A Shamanic Approach to Story took first place in the International Book Awards Writing/Publishing category. ***Phantastic Fiction*** is Matt's guide to dramatic writing that grew out of his popular Phantastic Fiction Workshop.

Night Whispers was an Award Winning Finalist in the Horror category of the International Book Awards. Set in the Boston neighborhood of Dorchester, ***Night Whispers*** is the story of Nick Powers, who loses consciousness after crashing in a stolen car and comes to hearing whispering voices in his mind. When he sees a homeless man arguing with himself, Nick realizes that the whispers in his head are the other side of the argument.

His memoir ***Spirit Matters*** detailing his journeys to Peru, working with shamanic plant medicines took first place in the San Diego Book Awards Spiritual Book Category, and was an Award-Winning Finalist in the autobiography/memoir category of the National Best Book Awards.

The Center Of The Universe Is Right Between Your Eyes But Home Is Where The Heart Is was an Award Winning Finalist in the International Book Awards. Based on a lifetime of research into shamanism, visionary states, the evolution of written communication and the roots of storytelling, award-winning author, editor, and shamanic explorer Matthew J. Pallamary takes those with open minds courageous enough to question the illusions that most of us think of as real on an expansive journey that pierces the veil of reality itself.

AfterLife: The Adventures of a Lost Soul was inspired by real life events, William Peter Blatty's ***The Exorcist***, and the dynamics of demonic possession.

Matt has also produced and directed ***The Santa Barbara Writers Conference Scrapbook*** documentary film and co-wrote the book of the same title in collaboration with Y. Armando Nieto, and conference founder Mary Conrad.

Death: (A Love Story) a first person narrative spoken by the omniscient voice of Death itself, who says, "I'm here to tell you stories and share some science, history, and myths, all of which are your creations that I want to share to help you understand me more. You have seen me as Satan, Anubis, Mot, Thanatos, God, the Devil, loving, punitive, dark, light – the list goes on and on! It is my sincerest hope that our friendly reintroduction here will change the way you think of me, and maybe in some small way reflect the depth of the love I have for you.

Picaflor is the sequel to ***Spirit Matters***, a San Diego Book Award winner and an Award-Winning Finalist in the National Best Book Awards that chronicles the two decades since of Matthew (Mateo) J. Pallamary's adventures in ***Spirit Matters*** through the mountains, deserts, and jungles of North, Central, and South America pursuing his studies of shamanism and visionary experience working with plant medicines and shamanic plant diets, among them Ayahuasca, Peyote, San Pedro cactus, and many more.

Picaflores: The Nerve Endings of GOD was an Award Winning Finalist in the International Book Awards that details a magical, otherworldly, intimate connection with the spirit of hummingbirds that comes from two decades of visionary journeys experienced within the context of shamanic plant diets in the Peruvian Amazon. It also contains a treasure trove of pre-Columbian myths about hummingbirds and an in-depth collection of amazing facts and figures about these magical creatures.

Holographicosmic Man: The Holographic Heart of the Golden Mean is an amalgam of quantum physics, mathematics, geometry, ancient texts, current research, ancient architecture, beliefs, and myths, astronomy, anthropology, human anatomy, brain structure, shamanism, neuroscience, neuropsychology, indigenous wisdom, astrophysics, neurophysiology, holography, neuroanatomy, neurocardiology, cosmometry, cosmology, biology, and more.

Matt's work has appeared in Oui, New Dimensions, The Iconoclast, Starbright, Infinity, Passport, The Short Story Digest, Redcat, The San Diego Writer's Monthly, Connotations, Phantasm, Essentially You, The Haven Journal, The Hurricanes & Swan Songs Anthology, The Santa Barbara Literary Journal, The Closed Eye Open, The Montecito Journal, and many others. His fiction has been featured in The San Diego Union Tribune which he has also reviewed books for, and his work has been heard on KPBS-FM in San Diego, KUCI FM in Irvine, television Channel Three in Santa Barbara, and The Susan Cameron Block Show in Vancouver. He has been a guest on the following nationally syndicated talk shows; Coast to Coast with George Noory, Paul Rodriguez, In The Light with Michelle

Whitedove, Susun Weed, Medicine Woman, Inner Journey with Greg Friedman, Night Dreams, and Environmental Directions Radio series. Matt has appeared on the following television shows; Bridging Heaven and Earth, Elyssa's Raw and Wild Food Show, Things That Matter, Literary Gumbo, Indie Authors TV, Spiritually Raw, and ECONEWS. He has also been a frequent guest on numerous podcasts, among them, The Psychedelic Salon, Black Light in the Attic, Third Eye Drops, C-Realm, Psychedelics Today, Voices in the Dark, Adventures Through the Mind, Beyond the Veil, Mind Escape, and many others.

Matt received the Man of the Year Award from San Diego Writer's Monthly Magazine and has taught a fiction workshop at the **Southern California Writers' Conference** in San Diego, Palm Springs, and Los Angeles, and at the **Santa Barbara Writers' Conference** for over thirty years. He has lectured at the Greater Los Angeles Writer's Conference, the Getting It Write conference in Oregon, the Saddleback Writers' Conference, the Rio Grande Writers' Seminar, the National Council of Teachers of English, The San Diego Writer's and Editor's Guild, The San Diego Book Publicists, The Pacific Institute for Professional Writing, The 805 Writers Conference, The College of Central Florida, Yakima Valley College in Washington, The Yakima Public School System, and he has been a panelist at the World Fantasy Convention, Con-Dor, and Coppercon. He is presently Editor in Chief of Mystic Ink Publishing.

Matt was a featured lecturer and performer at the **Mysteries of the Amazon** exhibit at the Appleton Museum in Ocala Florida and The Larson Gallery in Yakima Washington. He frequently visits the mountains, deserts, and jungles of North, Central, and South America pursuing his studies of shamanism.

MATTPALLAMARY.COM

BOOKS BY MATTHEW J. PALLAMARY

THE SMALL DARK ROOM OF THE SOUL

LAND WITHOUT EVIL

SPIRIT MATTERS

DREAMLAND (WITH KEN REETH)

THE INFINITY ZONE (WITH PAUL MAYBERRY)

A SHORT WALK TO THE OTHER SIDE

CYBERCHRIST

EYE OF THE PREDATOR

PHANTASTIC FICTION

NIGHT WHISPERS

THE SANTA BARABARA WRITERS CONFERENCE SCRAPBOOK (WITH MARY CONRAD & Y. ARMANDO NIETO)

n0THING

AFTERLIFE: THE ADVENTURES OF A LOST SOUL

THE CENTER OF THE UNIVERSE IS RIGHT BETWEEN YOUR EYES BUT HOME IS WHERE THE HEART IS

DEATH: (A LOVE STORY)

PICAFLOR

PICAFLORES: THE NERVE ENDINGS OF GOD

HOLOGRAPHICOSMIC MAN

THE THINNING VEIL

www.ingramcontent.com/pod-product-compliance
Lightning Source LLC
LaVergne TN
LVHW010919110826
845149LV00013B/2425

* 9 7 9 8 9 8 8 4 9 9 8 3 1 *